£4.95

GW00975925

THE LEAVES OF THE TREE

A CHRISTIAN APPROACH
TO HEALTH AND WHOLENESS

AN ANTHOLOGY WRITTEN

AND COMPILED BY

JOHN BANKS

MOORLEY'S Print & Publishing

British Library Cataloguing in Publication Data.
A catalogue record for this book is available
from the British Library.

ISBN 0 86071 558 2

MOORLEY'S Print & Publishing
23 Park Rd., Ilkeston, Derbys DE7 5DA
✄ Tel/Fax: (0115) 932 0643 ✄

2

CONTENTS

INTRODUCTION
THE LEAVES OF THE TREE

We all need the healing touch of Christ. To our dying day we are all damaged people in need of His wholeness.

We must not departmentalise the sick. We need to include ourselves among them. The damage may be in our mental health, tendency to worry, anxiety, fear, mood swings, obsessions or phobias. It may be some physical problem or handicap. It may be some emotional hurt that we've carried from the past. It may be some ingrained fault or sense of guilt. Perhaps it is a prejudiced attitude or an unforgiving spirit which eats away inside us like a cancer. It could be some major disappointment or frustration. It could be self-centredness which blocks our links with God and people.

As a discerning French doctor put it, "There are no sicknesses, only sick people."

We can be physically fit but inwardly sick. On the other hand we can be very sick, but inwardly, in our personality, well on the way to wholeness.

In Revelation, the final book of the Bible, John, the author, foresees final healing, real wholeness, for all who trust God, in life beyond death. He says of the tree of life that "the leaves of the tree are for the healing of the nations" (NIV Revelation 22 v.2).

There is corporate healing as well as personal healing – just as we speak now of world health and community health as well as individual health.

Clearly we have many foretastes of God's wholeness **now.** Think of the many who are being healed in their personality, at one with God, with people and life in general. Think of the healing that has come to South Africa following the collapse of the evils of apartheid. Much forgiveness has gone into that, from Nelson Mandela, Archbishop Desmond Tutu and others. Forgiveness is a real healing ingredient in life. Archbishop Desmond Tutu's recent book 'No future without forgiveness' is a moving testimony to the truth of that. He has gone to Northern Ireland and Rwanda with the same message.

The tree of health and wholeness draws its moisture from God, described in Ezekiel 47 and Revelation 22 as a river. All healing comes from God even if some of its agents do not acknowledge this.

This anthology is drawn up to show that there is a wider variety of leaves on this tree of God's ministry of health and wholeness than we realise. There are therapies that we could benefit from more than we think. There is an over-all unity. I believe it is helpful to bring several of these therapies together in an over-all view.

Medical science provides some very important leaves but not the only ones. There are leaves of health and wholeness provided by authentic complementary medicine, and by ministries such as friendship, forgiveness, reconciliation, peace-making, music, humour, prayer, Holy Communion, counselling, the Bible, truth and pastoral care.

This anthology is an attempt to give something of the range of some leaves on this tree. God clearly uses them in the total ministry of health and wholeness. Often this basic point is over-looked and sadly some people polarise the issues.

God is working through both the medical and the spiritual. We sometimes forget this. At times we feel that God isn't answering our prayers. We fail to see how wide-ranging is His help for us, much of it channelled through people. So it is good to bring together within one anthology some of these therapies through which God is working to help us to tackle our adversities. There is food for thought here both for sufferers and for carers. Therefore hopefully it will help many people.

Sometimes in situations of greatest need God can seem far away but the Cross and Resurrection mean that He is there holding on to us and very often working through people and prayer. Often we only realise this later as we look back.

The ministry of health and wholeness is not to be confused with faith healing. That wrongly gives the impression that when there is sufficient faith there can be the expectancy of physical cure. As we realise from experience some of the most lovely faithful Christian people often do not get better physically, but can have a deep inner wholeness in their personality. That is the most important healing of all.

God cannot be manipulated. He seeks to share in our suffering through the Cross, giving us love, courage and inner strength. Sometimes there is physical betterness as well. Why this is so in some people but not in others remains a mystery beyond our understanding. However Christians do not see death as defeat but as the entrance to fuller life through the Resurrection. The Bible assures us that in the future life there is no more suffering.

In an article in '*The Times*' newspaper some years ago Bishop Russell Barry wrote these words: "The Creator's love suffers with his children. Christian experience has affirmed that nothing, life or death, things present or things to come, can separate us from the love of God which is in Christ Jesus our Lord ... light which illuminates the mystery and shines unquenched in the hour of darkness."

God is **in** the suffering with us – not aloof from it nor willing it upon us – but giving us the love and courage to cope with it all.

Thankfully there are signs that many nowadays in medical and Church circles see the importance of medical and spiritual care being brought together. For example the eminent doctor Sir James Watt sees the value of inter-disciplinary team-work in patient care, and mentions for instance the value of counselling skills. He has also pointed out that seeing medicine in a very secular way is comparatively recent in human history. Ancient civilisations realised that there were spiritual factors in much illness, and so they had a wholeness approach to it – namely seeing the inter-connection of body, mind and spirit.

Bishop Morris Maddocks, a leading authority in the Church on medical-spiritual links sees this theme of wholeness as offering a constructive way forward in this whole sphere. Many medics are convinced Christians and others also appreciate the spiritual factors in health issues.

Doctors are not just dealing with cases, but with people. My own excellent doctor for many years recalls seeing a motto in a consultant's office, words of Ambrose Pare about the role of the doctor, "I tended him, God healed him."

The role of medicine is splendidly described by Dr. Paul Tournier in this way: "It has been said of medicine that its duty is sometimes to heal, often to afford relief, and always to bring consolation. This is exactly what the Bible tells us that God does for suffering humanity. Sometimes God heals, but not always. But He gives relief, He protects and sustains us in times of affliction: and His consolation is unending. Here too we may say that the doctor in his vocation works hand in hand with God."[1]

The key role of the Christian faith is wonderfully expressed by Bishop Russell Barry, who himself went through much suffering, in an article in 'The Times' in July 1970:-

"One of the strongest claims of Christianity is that it faces the mystery of pain without sentimentality or evasion. It never tries to pretend that it does not hurt. It offers no superficial consolations. It points to One who suffered and died and rose again, who 'has borne our griefs and carried our sorrows,' and through them offers healing and victory. The pattern of the Cross and Resurrection is woven into the fabric of man's existence."

Christians need to show the world that Christ's presence makes all the difference, so that people can see that in Him all things find their real meaning, indeed their salvation.

---

[1] Paul Tournier 'A Doctor's Casebook in the light of the Bible', S.C.M. Press 1954.

ACKNOWLEDGEMENTS

I wish to thank warmly those who have so helpfully written articles for this Anthology:-

Dr. Tony Short, formerly Director of the Clinical Laboratory, University Hospital Medical School, Nottingham.

Rev. David Howell, formerly Adviser for the Ministry of Health and Healing, Bath & Wells Diocese.

Rev. David Payne, formerly Warden of Crowhurst.

Mrs. Vivienne Pearson, Chartered Physiotherapist.

Rev. John Wardle, formerly Vicar Choral of Southwell Minster and Adviser for the Ministry of Health & Healing, Southwell Diocese; now Rector of Bridlington Priory.

Rev. Canon Philip Humphreys, formerly Rector of St. Giles West Bridgford, Nottingham and Music Therapist with those with learning disabilities.

Rev. Martin Kerry, Team Leader, The Chaplaincy, Nottingham City Hospital.

Mr. Alan Langton, formerly Head Teacher, Southwolds Comprehensive School, Keyworth, Nottinghamshire.

Rev. Ken Evans, a Psychotherapist: my thanks to him for permission to quote extensively from an article written when he was Anglican Chaplain of the Mental Illness Unit, Nottingham. Director Sherwood Psychotherapy Training Institute

I am also grateful to Dr. Cicely Saunders, Mrs. Grace Sheppard, the Rev. Barrie Newton, Bishop Morris Maddocks and Mrs. Jane Grayshon to quote from their writings.

Rev. Barrie Cooke, Senior Consultant of the Bible Society for the use of some selected material from an article published in the Methodist Health and Healing Magazine 1992.

I grateful to Hodder and Stoughton Ltd for permission to reproduce verses from the NIV Bible and some other quotations.

Many thanks also to my wife Sue for kindly typing the manuscript and for her helpful comments, and for Tony and Brenda Blades for helping on the computer.

I am grateful to the publishers and authors who have given me permission to use quotations. I have tried to contact all my sources and apologise for any inadvertent omissions which will be rectified in any reprint.

CHAPTER ONE

RELEASE THROUGH HUMOUR

There was a very moving programme on television about Harry Secombe's steady recovery following a severe stroke. It would give hope and encouragement to patients and carers.

The obvious physical and emotional downsides of the stroke were realistically faced and shining through the difficulties were the Christian strengths of faith and humour. Medical and spiritual strength have been very helpful to Harry. He said, "I know that my Redeemer liveth." Then he went onto say, "I'm in God's hands. God has got a very safe pair of hands." This was followed by Harry's humorous chuckle, "God would make a very good wicket-keeper!"

Humour is a great releaser of tension and pent-up feelings. It helps us to smile. It helps us to be more serene and so is beneficial to health. It's an important leaf in the tree of health and wholeness.

There is a lot of humour in the Bible, in both Old and New Testaments. Some of it is inadvertent. In College days a friend of mine was situated in a room near to some bathrooms. At night time he was often disturbed by the noise of people taking a late bath. Psalm 42 verse 9 was on his mind, "One deep calleth another, because of the noise of the water-pipes!"

There is much humour in the witty book of Jonah. Jonah clearly lacked a sense of humour, but the author used humour to drive home the point that in life we are called to share faith in God. This is for our wholeness. Jonah travels off in the opposite direction. When God gives him a second chance he sulks. However, he feels sorry for the plant withered by the sun. God says can't Jonah see **His** sorrow for people who have never found their way in life. The last verse of the book is a masterly touch of humour (Jonah 4 verse 11).

Jesus clearly had a lovely sense of humour. He enjoyed parties and felt at ease in them without compromising his principles. His comments on forgiveness are very witty. He points to the ridiculous way some people in their quest for a speck in someone's eye, a minor fault, miss the major fault, the plank in their own eye (Matthew 7 v.1-5). So an important point is made about forgiveness, which is a healing ingredient, through humour.

We tend not to appreciate how important a sense of humour is in the pursuit of health and wholeness. Not only is it a safety valve releasing a lot of pent-up frustrations and anxieties, but also it stops us taking ourselves too seriously.

"Give us a sense of humour, Lord, and also things to laugh about. Give us the grace to take a joke against ourselves, and to see the funny side of life."[2]

Humour gives us a sense of proportion. Malcolm Sargent, the famous conductor, who went through much suffering, in a broadcast spoke of the need for a sense of humour. He said, "It means placing a relative value on oneself, so that even in one's greatest tragedy there's still something that makes one smile."[3]

There is a lot of medical evidence for the beneficial effects of laughter. Harry Williams points out in his book '*Tensions*' (Fount 1989) that laughter is a sign of our feeling accepted by God – it is this ability to laugh at ourselves and in an unhurtful way to laugh at others. This helps in the healing of relationships, one of the most important aspects of healing.

In our care for others we can sometimes be gentle with them and hard on ourselves. We need to be more gentle with ourselves and a sense of humour helps in this. As a wise psychotherapist said to me, "Remember, John, we are all part of flawed humanity."

Again and again Jesus was encouraging his followers with the words "Fear not." On one recorded occasion he added, "In the world you will have tribulation but be of good cheer, I have overcome the world."

Joy is second in St. Paul's list of the fruits of the Spirit (Galatians 5 verse 22). It is a good advertisement for our Christian faith and a sign of our growth towards being made whole.

Medics use the term 'placebo', meaning 'I shall please' for medication that has no medical value. The patients think it's helping them and so in fact it is beneficial.

A lot of humour comes in everyday conversation as comedians such as Ronnie Barker, Tommy Cooper and Al Read showed. It is even funnier when it is unintentional, and can be a tonic even in sad situations.

A clergy colleague was returning from a cremation. He was alone in the hearse with the undertaker. It was the curate's first visit to that particular crematorium. He asked if it was open for cremations on a Saturday morning. "Oh no," said the undertaker solemnly – "Just Monday

---

[2] From a prayer by A.G. Bullivant (in New Parish Prayers ed. by Frank Colquhoun, Hodder & Stoughton).

[3] Malcolm Sargent by Charles Reid p.330 Hodder & Stoughton.

to Friday. Just a minute, I think one at Doncaster does open, but I believe they only have a skeleton staff on duty!"

Christian faith is the greatest antidote to the fear of death which afflicts so many people.

Easter faith is the key – and humour also helps. This reminds me of the story of the cricketing enthusiast who said to his local Vicar one day, "Do you think there'll be cricket in heaven, Vicar?" The Vicar had a sense of humour and said he would think about it. They met again a few days later. The Vicar said, "I've got good news for you and sad news. First the good news. Yes, I think there will be cricket in heaven. Now the sad news. You're picked for next Saturday!"

Another sporting story in relation to fear of death and the burden of a troubled conscience is as follows. A Scottish rugby player scored a try, in an international match. He realised in his conscience that it wasn't really a try because the referee didn't see that he had 'knocked the ball on' as it was passed to him. Ever after it troubled him to think of it. When he got to the gates of heaven he was still burdened. He saw an apostle standing there and took it to be St. Peter. He said to him that he'd got to come clean and own up. The apostle reassured him. "Don't worry about it any more. You see, I'm St. Andrew. It's St. Peter's day off today!"

Some of the fear of death can thus be melted by humour even if it's not always very tactful. An undertaker telephoned me to tell me about a funeral. I said, "Will it be before the week-end?" "Oh no," he said fervently – "they're as busy as blazes at the crematorium!" It was hardly a delicate reply!

Sometimes humour can have a surprise element which can warm the heart. In hospital chaplaincy work, we sometimes have theological students doing practical training. One of them said to me, "You'll need to go and visit Mrs. So-and-so, she's very depressed and suicidal." I went, and to my surprise found her quite perky. She said, "I've had a trainee parson come to see me. He seemed a bit down, so I said a prayer for him"!

I am sure God has a sense of humour and would have smiled warmly at the following incident. I was ministering Holy Communion to a group of elderly patients in a hospital day-room. One little old lady was sitting near the group. I was anxious to ensure she was not missed out and asked if she would like Holy Communion. Back came here reply, "I'd rather have a cup of tea!"

One of the most refreshing Christian leaders I have met was Bishop Richard Darby, who was much loved during his ministry in Nottinghamshire. He had been through great suffering in World War 2 as a prisoner of war in Japanese hands. Through the suffering he came to trust even more our suffering Saviour, Jesus. His preaching on this was very moving. You felt he'd really lived the meaning of the Cross and Resurrection. He also had a tremendous sense of humour. At a Stewardship Supper he told the story of a boy who swallowed a penny. The parents tried several avenues of help to recover the penny from the boy's inside – doctor, hospital etc., but in vain. Then the father had a brainwave. He said, "We'll take him to the Vicar – he can get money out of anybody!"

Bishop Russell Barry, a former Bishop of Southwell, was revered in his own life-time, a great man with a wonderful mind. His humour also shone through much suffering. He won the D.S.O. as a brave Chaplain in World War 1, whilst rescuing wounded soldiers from the battlefield. In World War 2 his home and church were destroyed in the blitz on London. He used to say that his faith had undergone many an hour of doubt and darkness, but that the darkness had not overcome it. It shone out serene amidst the suffering. He had a ready wit and could administer a salutary rebuke in a telling way. A rather self-opinionated preacher waffled on in a sermon. The Bishop who was slumped in his chair was heard to mutter audibly as the preacher descended the pulpit steps, "Rather a wasted effort!"

Again and again in our experience we see how God works mainly through people. The research of people like Bishop John Finney in "Finding Faith Today" shows that most people come into a settled Christian faith through personal contacts. In the medical sphere there are obviously many people with considerable gifts of healing. Whether they are believers or not they are God's agents in this sphere.

Children can readily grasp this truth of God working through people. For example a small child in a loud voice prayed that God would bring him a big box of chocolates for his birthday. His mother said, "Don't shout, God isn't deaf." "No", said the boy, "but Grandpa is, and he's in the next room!"[4]

Children can grasp too the dangers to life and limb through foolish behaviour. A Sunday School teacher was instructing her class about the dangers of looking back. She explained to them that Lot's wife looked back and turned into a pillar of salt. A little girl in the class piped up, "My Mum looked back when she was driving the car so she could see a friend's new house, and she turned into a lamp-post!"

---

[4] Derek Nimmo, 'Oh, Come on, all ye Faithful.' Robson Books.

Children can also wind us up. They realise they're doing it. A little boy clearly recognised this as the following conversation shows. He was asked at Sunday School, "Do you say your prayers at night?" He said, "No, Mummy does it for me. She says, 'Thank God, you're in bed at last!'"[5]

One of the healing features of present day Christianity is the way the Churches are growing closer together for the Kingdom of God. Good examples of this are in Hospital Chaplaincy work, and the areas of ecumenical experiment in parish life. Some of the healing comes through our being readier to smile at ourselves more. This comes out in the following joke about some Anglicans who were at a Conference Centre in the countryside. They were on a walk and came across a very rickety bridge over a fast flowing stream. It had a warning sign on it. Foolishly they were about to try to cross it when an irate farmer came across them and shouted "Who do you think you are?" "We're Anglicans from the local Centre," they replied. "If you don't look out," replied the farmer, "you'll soon all be Baptists!"

Hardness of hearing has its humour. A very frail old lady was being questioned by a social worker. She asked, "Are you incontinent?" The old lady was hard of hearing and replied, "Oh yes, I've been many times to the Continent! I've even been to Australia!" She was tickled pink about it when she realised her error of hearing. There is much humour in medical situations even in matters of life and death. A friend went to see a hospital Consultant for a check up following a major operation. The doctor was very poker faced. He said solemnly, "I am prescribing some medication for you. You will need to be on this medication for the rest of your life. I am giving you a week's supply!" My friend burst out laughing and only then did the doctor realise the implication of the way he'd expressed it, and laughed too.

A famous Scottish preacher has said that Joy is the flag that flies from the heart when the King of Kings is in residence." It is deeper than happiness. As someone has put it, "Happiness happens, joy abides." Joy is the deeper inner sense of experiencing the presence of God, so we can have joy even in dark days. It is no accident that the first of the signs of Jesus's nature as both God and man was made clear at the joy of a village wedding – the Wedding at Cana.

There is a sense of humour shown in Christ's conversation with the Syro-Phoenician woman as recorded in St. Mark's Gospel chapter 7, and St. Matthew chapter 15. There is laughter and repartee. At first Jesus does not answer the woman's request for healing for her daughter. The disciples want him to send her away. Jesus makes it clear that his earthly

---

[5] Ibid.Nimmo.

15

ministry is firstly directed towards Israel, though of course it is for the whole world. Then he says to the woman, "It is not right to take the children's bread and to toss it to their dogs" (Mark 7 verse 27 NIV). Christopher Hamel Cook in 'The Language of Joy' (Arthur James) points out that the word he uses here is better translated 'little dogs' or even 'puppies'. The woman joins in the banter. Jesus commends her response. The daughter is healed.

Humour can come in worship, even when there is stress. A Vicar friend was conducting a Family Service and as he was giving his talk a toddler became increasingly fractious. The mother, all hot and bothered, tried to calm her but to no avail. In despair she picked up the toddler and started to leave the service. The Vicar called out, "Please don't go. She's not bothering me." "No," replied the mother, "but you're bothering her!" There's no answer to that!

A SMILE COSTS NOTHING, but gives much.
It enriches those who receive, without making poorer those who give.
It takes but a moment, but the memory of it sometimes lasts for ever.
None is so rich or mighty that he can get along without it, and none is so poor but that he cannot be made rich by it.
A smile creates happiness in the home, fosters goodwill in business, and is the countersign of friendship.
It brings rest to the weary, cheer to the discouraged, sunshine to the sad, and it is nature's best antidote for trouble.
Yet it cannot be bought, begged or borrowed, for it is something that is of no value to anyone until it is given away.
Some people are too tired to give you a smile.
Give them one of yours, as none needs a smile so much as he who has no more to give.   *Anon.*

CHAPTER TWO

PRAYING HANDS

Prayer is not something we initiate but something into which we enter. As a well-known hymn puts it:-

As o'er each continent and island
The dawn leads on another day
The voice of prayer is never silent
Nor dies the strain of praise away.
J. Ellerton.

Across the world prayer is being offered to God around the clock. Tennyson wrote:-

"More things are wrought by prayer
Than this world dreams of" *(Idyll of the King).*

As C. S. Lewis says in the film 'Shadowlands', "Prayer does not change God but it changes me."

God's will for us is constant love. We have to let our minds be so transformed by prayer that we are tuned into God's will, and aligned with it. As we pray that God's will may be done in others and in ourselves, they and we can experience inner peace even if outward afflictions remain. Some patients tell me of being fearful before an operation, but sense an inner peace coming when they know that people are praying for them.

Prayer is not just saying prayers, whether written or extempore. Prayer is an attitude of heart and mind, consciously turning our ordinary everyday experiences towards God. Then we are gradually moving towards the point where all of life becomes prayer. So we are strengthened along the journey towards wholeness, and are a blessing to others.

As Mother Teresa put it: "Offer to God every movement you make. He will use you to accomplish great things on condition that you believe much more in His love than in your own weakness." As we walk down the street, and pass a health centre or a hospital, or a nursing home, just turn them in your thoughts towards God. "A prayer in its simplest definition is merely a wish turned Godward" (Phillips Brooks).

Similarly when you are watching the television or reading the newspaper turn the people and events mentioned there towards God. We need to read our newspapers prayerfully as well as our Bibles. As we see a passing ambulance turn the crew and patient in our thoughts towards God.

We need to be on the look-out to see God in people, the child on the Christian Aid appeal or the courageous face of the sufferer. As Mother Teresa said: "To be able to see God in each other we need an open heart, and an open heart is achieved by prayer."

To pray in the name of Jesus is to pray in the character of Jesus. This means we face realities in His strength and don't try to run away from them. We can shoot up little arrow prayers to God, for example, that of the poet and pastor, George Herbert, "Thou hast given us so much, give one thing more, a thankful heart."

Michel Quoist's 'Prayers of Life' help us to see the way in which the whole of life can be turned into prayer. When he sees a telephone Michel Quoist is reminded that prayer should be two-way traffic between us and God, listening and talking.

"Since I didn't listen, I didn't help,
Since I didn't listen, we didn't communicate."[6]

We can absorb a lot of God's love in silent prayer. A French priest went into church and found a humble villager gazing into space in silence. The priest asked him what he was doing. The villager replied, "He looks at me and I look at Him, and we're happy together." Such union with God in contemplative prayer is inner health-giving.

We need to pray especially in the name of Jesus expecting that God will work through our prayers, though not always according to what we want, but always to what is needed. As William Carey, the Northamptonshire shoe-maker and famous missionary said, "Expect great things from God, attempt great things for God."

People are hungry for love. The essence of God's nature is love, as demonstrated through His human form in Jesus and the Holy Spirit at work in our lives. The sick do not want pity. They want love. "God is still love. He is still loving the world. Today God loves the world so much that he gives you and He gives me to be His love and compassion."[7] This is how we can strengthen the sick and sorrowful.

Part of the ministry to the sick is the art of listening. We need to refrain from talking too much when we visit the sick. Mother Teresa also emphasises the importance of listening in the quietness:-

"We need silence to be able to touch souls. See how nature, the trees, the flowers, the grass grow in perfect silence – see the stars, the moon and

---

[6] Prayers of Life. Gill p.15.

[7] Mother Teresa

the sun, how they move in silence. The more we receive in silent prayer, the more we can give in our active life. We need silence to be able to touch souls. The essential thing is not what we say but what God says through us."

Prayer with Thanksgiving

The sense of thankfulness lifts our minds away from self and worries and up to God and outwards to the needs of others. Such thankful prayer therefore helps promote health and wholeness. G.K. Chesterton said of the atheist, that "his worst moment is when he is really thankful and has no one to thank."

"Do not be anxious about anything, but in everything, by prayer and petition with thanksgiving present your requests to God. And the peace of God, which transcends all understanding will guard your hearts and your minds in Christ Jesus" (St. Paul, Philippians 4 v.6-7 NIV).

"We all ought to make an effort to act on our first thoughts and let our unspoken gratitude find expression. Then there will be more sunshine in the world, and more power to work for what is good" (Dr. Albert Schweitzer).

We remember how Jesus through his ministry recorded in the Gospels, had compassion on people who were sick in body, mind and spirit, and turned that compassion into prayer and action.

> May your presence be with them
> to relieve suffering and distress
> and to restore them to fullness of life
> for your great love's sake. Amen.[8]

Prayer reminds us that at the end of our own resources we are at the beginning of God's.

When we pray for the sick we need to pray what is best for them in the love of God. Also in our prayers we need to bring together the medical and the spiritual.

Children can grasp this point well and have a lovely candour in their approach which comes over well in the following child's prayer:-

"Dear God, please take care of us, and take care of yourself because without you we're sunk. Amen."

Children also have insight into the way that God works through people to answer our prayers. While I was working as a hospital chaplain, a

---

[8] Frank Colquhoun from a prayer for the sick – Contemporary Parish Prayers. Hodder and Stoughton.

young mother told me of a perceptive comment made by her small daughter. The child said, "Mum, God does answer prayers. He answers prayers by putting thoughts in other people's minds." What a wonderful description of intercessory prayer! This is very therapeutic, in prayer bringing people into the presence of Jesus.

We cannot bring anyone physically into the presence of Jesus as the four people did in Mark 2, but we can bring them into His healing presence through prayer.

Christ is timeless so He can deal with all inner feelings, past and present. Prayer can open all this up as the following prayer of that great person of prayer, Bishop George Appleton makes clear in the following:-

"O Spirit of God,
Set at rest the crowded, hurrying conscious thoughts
Within our minds and hearts.
Let the peace and quiet of your presence take possession of us.
Help us to relax, to rest, to become open and receptive to you.
You know our inmost spirits,
the hidden unconscious life within us,
the forgotten memories of hurts and fears,
the frustrated desires,
the unresolved tensions and dilemmas
Cleanse and sweeten the springs of our being
that freedom, life and love may flow
into both our conscious and hidden life.
Lord, we lie open before you, waiting for healing,
Your peace and your word. Amen."

(Quoted by permission of his literary Executor).

CHAPTER THREE

HEALING TOUCH

It is good when we go to a concert with a piano concerto as a main work to have a seat with a view of the keyboard. Then we can see the touch of the pianist – a master touch.

Touch is a key factor in wide-ranging situations. A sign of welcome, friendship or congratulations to someone is to shake hands.

When we go to visit a friend in adversity we clasp their hand and thereby establish a bond of compassion and understanding, a sign of God's care for them. This action speaks louder than words.

We speak of inward touch also. For example we speak of being greatly touched by a message of encouragement.

Any of us who are parents know what a touch given in love can express to our children. The living Jesus offers to all His touch of love upon our lives, a master touch that we all need because we are all to a degree damaged people.

An increasing number of churches have the ministry of laying-on-of-hands with prayer, and anointing with oil, through which God's strength comes to us through touch as well as words as it did in Bible times.

"In an age of high and sophisticated technology the gentle human touch of the hands of the doctor, the nurse, the priest, the carer, the helper or the friend, is needed as perhaps never before."[9]

It is clear from the New Testament that in his earthly ministry of health and wholeness, Jesus used touch as well as words. "A man with leprosy came to him and begged him on his knees, 'If you are willing, you can make me clean.' Filled with compassion, Jesus reached out his hand and touched the man. 'I am willing,' he said, 'Be clean!' Immediately the leprosy left him and he was cured" (Mark 1 v.40-42 NIV). For other examples see also Mark 1 v.31, Luke 5 v.12, Luke 8 v.44, Matthew 20 v.34.

Jesus touching or being touched implies a holding as the Greek verb used makes clear. This ministry of touch brought much reassurance and helped to remove fear. It conveyed God's love. In the Acts of the Apostles there are six occasions recorded when touch is used, two including 'the laying-on-of-hands'. Ananias lays his hands on Saul of

---

[9] Norman Autton, 'Touch – an Exploration.' Darton, Longman & Todd p.141.

Tarsus in his blindness (Acts 9 verses 17-19) and in Acts 28 Paul ministers to the father of Publius, ill with fever, through the 'laying-on-of-hands'. The healthy use of touch can help to reduce distance between people. When someone is in distress, to clasp their hand can convey more effectively than words our compassionate care for them.

In the Service of laying-on-of-hands the ministrant is not acting as an individual, but as representative of the whole Church. Their prayers and pastoral care are important back-up. Very humbly we are conscious of the hands of God working through our frail hands. A typical prayer at a Service of laying-on-of-hands might be this:- "May Almighty God, Father, Son and Holy Spirit, make you whole in body, mind and spirit, protect you from all that harms you and give you His light and peace. May the Risen Jesus in all His love reach out to you with His healing touch and help you more and more to be a channel of His love and prayer for others. For His dear Name's sake. Amen."

"The hands of God" is a very expressive way of describing God's care. As Jesus Himself says, "My sheep listen to my voice; I know them and they follow me. I give them eternal life, and they shall never perish; no-one can snatch them out of my hand" (John 10 v.27-28 NIV).

Faith is not so much our holding on to God, but trusting that He is holding on to us.

"Faith is the constant putting of ourselves into his hands. The reward of faith is that we are kept by Him and have nothing else to fear."[10]

> 'Let me no more my comfort draw
> From my frail hold of Thee;
> In this alone rejoice with awe
> Thy mighty grasp of me!'

When our frail human hands are given to the service of God, then He can work sensitively through them for the well-being of others. "When an outward and human touch becomes transformed by an inward and divine love, it is then, and then only, that we are able to bring solace to the sad, strength to the weak, and healing to the sick."[11]

The Christian community called L'Arche working with mentally handicapped adults in France, sings a hymn, entitled "The Hands of God".

> The hands of God have been laid upon our sorrowful faces;
> The hands of God have caressed our wounded hearts
> Giving relief, at last, from the flames of suffering,
> Will our hands be laid in this way too?[12]

---

[10] Douglas Webster, 'In Debt to Christ'. P.61 Highway Press.

[11] Autton ibid. p.141.

[12] Published in Touch by Norman Autton, Darton, Longman & Todd

One of the impressive ways that Princess Diana showed her empathy with the sick, maimed and disadvantaged, was through her sensitive ministry of touch.

"I believe that most of us, when we are sick, need physical contact and the spoken assurance of God's love."[13]

A prayerful touch can be very meaningful. The laying-on-of-hands with prayer is a formalising, in a service, of this basic instinct to care and share.

"Jesus used the simple touch. There was nothing magical in this. I often wish we could find a phrase other than the 'laying-on-of-hands', for all it really means is the 'touch of Christ', who in His compassion and power shares and heals."[14]

The patient is drawn more closely into the body of Christ. As Bishop Morris Maddocks points out God is able to use this act to enfold us into His Son's health-giving body. The sufferer receives that touch through the body. So it carries theological and psychological value.

"The use of touch in both massage and physiotherapy can be a comforting and therapeutic agent: stress can be reduced, muscular aches and pains soothed, joints unlocked and a feeling of well-being gained."[15]

Here is a description by a Chartered Physiotherapist of her work:-

PHYSIOTHERAPY IN HEALTH AND WHOLENESS

Touch gives the full picture of the body – far more than can be seen by the eye. Shape and bulk of joints, tendons, ligaments, muscle and bone can be appreciated and defined by touch. Stress and tension also become "visible" through the fingers in altered muscle tone, changed postural reactions and pain response. This knowledge of the body and its working can then be translated into healing, be it advice and exercise the patient commits to use at home, or the physical treatments of manipulation, massage and electrotherapy, or any combination of the two.

From time to time, everyone develops problems. Like our cars and bicycles, bodies need regular attention to keep them going mechanically, but as we are delivered without "log-books", we don't always attend to this.

So how can we direct our health and well-being?

The first consideration is to keep ourselves in tip-top condition. Age is no barrier. Nine or ninety-nine, we can deal with our physical problems as they arise, not waiting for the "right time" to come

---

[13] Michael Mayne, former Dean of Westminster Abbey, 'A Year lost and found', 1987.
[14] George Bennett 'The Heart of Healing' p.48 Arthur James.
[15] Norman Autton 'Touch' p.129 DLT.

along when there is a space in our lives for us to use. General aches and pains can often be helped by gentle exercise and stretching. Posture can be improved and work positions examined – in the home or in the employment environment. You can take advice and treatment by physical means, but the control of the situation is yours. Deal with these aches and pains as they arise to keep your physical well-being to an optimum.

Specific injuries or problems can be diagnosed and targeted.

Tension and stress are common factors in all our lives, keeping us motivated and ready to give of our best. These body states are part of our normal balance. Sometimes, this balance is disturbed and we become what has become known as 'stressed'. Speaking from a personal point of view, the use of touch is an integral part of looking at the whole person. Tension can be felt by gentle manipulation of muscles and soft tissues. It is necessary to be able to recognise when we are stressed, and we all show it in different ways. The tightness produced by stress puts our whole body out of balance, and can lead to physical symptoms. For example, tension of the muscles around the neck and shoulders quickly occurs when we are anxious or working hard. This in turn makes the joints more difficult to move, and pain ensues. The pain changes our posture, throwing strain onto other areas, and there we are with pain in other parts of our bodies as well. It is important to break this cycle as soon as possible.

Seek help about the initial pain. Then, if you or your doctor or therapist recognise stress as a cause, learn relaxation techniques. Massage is a great de-stress mechanism = slow rhythmical movements relaxing body and mind. Acupuncture is another ancient art that can play a true role in relaxation. If you feel reluctant to seek help, there are good books and cassettes around to help you practise relaxation, written by professionals and available from most book shops.

Exercise can also form part of your anti-stress strategy. Activity is vital to life. At nine you may play football every day, at ninety-nine, it takes more thinking about. However, as we get older, that walk upstairs or down to the shops is valid exercise. Take time to walk the dog, or just walk and relax with friends.

We owe it to ourselves to "keep fit for life". We owe it to those around us to have the strength and vigour to tread this path through life, and in our well - being, we can reach out and touch others encouraging them to make the same journey. (Vivienne Pearson).

At its simplest the laying-on-of-hands is not a formal ministry at all. Visiting a sick person in hospital one naturally takes him by the hand or the shoulder, or lays a hand on his forehead when praying with him. It is an effective sign of identification with another person or special designation of the one for whom prayer is made. It gives a context of love to prayer.   *("Liturgy for the sick" p.21)*

CHAPTER FOUR

THE HANDS OF FRIENDSHIP

True friends are those who realise what we're really like, warts and all, and still love us and stand by us.

In an age when so many things have sexual overtones imposed upon them, it is important that we re-establish the genuineness of true friendship. It is a healing ingredient in life – described in the Book of Ecclesiasticus as 'a medicine of life'.

Illness and other adversity often provides a good test of true friendship. There are surprises too. Some that you think would rally to you keep their distance. Some surprise you by the depths of their concern. I remember being in hospital following a heart attack. One day a dark over-coated gentleman from a local firm of undertakers arrived on the ward to visit me, not with flowers (!) but with a lovely basket of fruit, and a helpful get well card. Obviously they were genuine and not looking for custom!

It was a very encouraging visit. True friendship does bring great encouragement and is an important leaf on the tree of healing. It helps us to feel valued – a therapy in itself.

There is a lot about friendship in the Bible. One of the most important friendships in the New Testament is the friendship of Paul and Luke. They were two people from completely contrasting backgrounds – but with a common bond of deep faith in Christ. Luke was clearly a big help to Paul in a medical capacity also. Being a doctor he must have understood the nature of Paul's recurrent illness – what Paul describes as 'a thorn in the flesh'. Some scholars think it may have been recurrent malaria; others feel it may have been an eye condition.

Luke obviously helped to encourage Paul on his arduous travels and demanding mission work. Paul describes him as 'our dear friend Luke the doctor' (Colossians 4 v.14). Paul writing from prison in 2 Timothy v.4 says 'Only Luke is with me'.

Both of them had a very out-going faith. That is clear from their writings. There is a healthiness about their outlook. Their wide concern is of God's love for all people, over-riding all man-made barriers. A

Christian doctor friend of ours in the early days of our marriage was a gynaecologist. When he knew we were expecting he said, "You'll look well if it's a double-yolker." He proved to be a prophet as well as a doctor friend. We had identical twins!

Jesus is our supreme friend as well as our Saviour. He makes this clear in His unconditional love for us and in His sayings. One particular saying of His to us at the Last Supper about this is recorded in St. John's Gospel chapter 15 – "No one has greater love than this, to lay down one's life for one's friends." Some of our truest friends come through Christian fellowship life. God not only gives us Himself, in Him we are given each other. Grace Sheppard suffered for many years from agrophobia and with medical and spiritual help came through her difficulties. As well as the loving support of her husband, David, then Bishop of Liverpool, she also gained much help from her friends.

The agrophobia produced in her deep fear – fear of losing control, of not being able to handle what might occur in life, and ultimately fear of death. Gradually with medical and spiritual help she came through these fears into new life.

Friendship was a factor in her healing. She writes about it in her book 'An Aspect of Fear' in this way:-

"Friendship is vital. So much of today's advertising and fiction focus on romantic love, that we have forgotten how important friendship is. Not only can friendship be the answer to loneliness, it can also provide the basis for creating a place where we can help each other to flourish and grow."[16]

"Finding a friend to trust, and who entrusts themselves to us is finding something very valuable and is to be treasured. Sharing our fears in this way is both healing and life-giving."[17]

The following description of friendship is well known:
"A friend is a person who is for you always. He wants nothing from you except that you be yourself. He is the one being with whom you can feel safe. With him you can utter your heart, its badness and its goodness. Like the shade of a great tree in the noonday heat is a friend. Like the home port with your country's flag flying

---

[16] Page 45, Darton, Longman and Todd.
[17] Ibid. p.46.

after a long journey is a friend. A friend is an impregnable citadel of refuge in the strife of existence. It is he that makes you believe that it is a good universe. He is the antidote to despair, the elixir of hope, the tonic for depression" (Anonymous).

A frequent remark made by people going through suffering, physical, mental or spiritual, is this, "I have discovered who are my real friends."

It is revealing when we are in any kind of difficulty to see who remains loyal and who keeps their distance. That has been my experience particularly during a long period of mental illness. Most people in any sort of trauma do not want to be pitied but to be loved, to be valued for what they are in themselves. To be affirmed as a person in the love of God is a great therapy in itself.

True friendship is one of the great ways in which God's love comes to us, God working through people to reach people. Real friends are people who understand our weaknesses as well as our strengths and yet love us none the less. I remember ministering to a family in bereavement and a young person expressing her grief and saying:- "You see Grandpa was a real friend. He loved me with an unconditional love." That of course is supremely the quality of God's love for us as the New Testament makes clear. True friends are people who are always there for us. That is one of the best therapies for those struggling with illness and other difficulties. Jesus, our supreme friend, is always true to his promise, "Remember I am with you always." Friends are people who have time for us, people who bring the best out in us and don't drag us down. One of the most important features of this quality of friendship is confidentiality. It is a bond of trust.

There should be one or two people in Christian fellowship life with whom we can share hopes and fears **confidentially.**

Friends often meet round a meal, and it is significant that the Christian fellowship life centres round a meal, the Holy Communion. We meet as friends round the Lord's table. As the verse of a hymn puts it:-

> "As Christ breaks bread for men to share,
> Each proud division ends.
> The love that made us, makes us one,
> And strangers now are friends" *(Brian A. Wren).*

Shared suffering brings its own particular quality of shared friendship. It is of course one of the things which makes our friendship with Jesus special, through the Cross.

Ernest Gordon has written a splendid book called "*Miracle on the River Kwai*" (Collins), a true story set in a Japanese prison camp in World War 2. Some of our troops there were brought through their shared sufferings into closer Christian friendship. They realised that faith would not save them from their plight, but that it would take them through it. Their experience was that suffering no longer locked them up in the grip of self-pity. It brought them out into what Dr. Albert Schweitzer calls 'the fellowship of those who bear the mark of pain, the fellowship of suffering humanity'.

This is another way we are brought along the road to wholeness. An ingredient in our inner healing, our wholeness of personality is the way in which Jesus, our wounded healer, inspires in us special qualities of friendship through shared suffering and other traumas.

It was my own experience during months of being a hospital patient that there can be supportive friendships formed. Even several non-committed Christians seemed to understand the particular torment to me, as a priest, that my illness brought. I shall always be grateful to them. It helped me to realise that God is at work outside the organised life of the Church as well as inside it. I find this very encouraging. I see it as one of the main tasks of the organised Churches to build bridges with those outside Church life who do pray, and have real spiritual insights and yearnings. It's good to have friends outside Church life as well as inside it.

Friendships within Church life have of course been of great blessing to me and to countless others. I recall the friendship we had with a newly married bride and her husband. They had gone forward courageously with the marriage although she was ill with cancer. Her Christian faith developed remarkably during the illness. Like many people I have met, as she grew physically weaker, she grew spiritually stronger.

Vanessa joined an adult group preparing for Confirmation and was a shining light amongst them. This influenced us all greatly. She was a powerful influence too amongst her friends at work.

She chose the Bible reading for her wedding. In that lesson came powerful words of St. Paul in Romans chapter 5, "Suffering produces perseverance, perseverance character, and character hope. And hope does not disappoint us, because God has poured out His love into our hearts by the Holy Spirit whom He has given us."

The friendship of children in suffering has a quality all of its own. It was a moving experience when I ministered in the mining parish of Ollerton to befriend a family when the youngest child who was eight years old was suffering from cancer. The reaction in that loving home could have been one of bitterness and despair. Instead it was positive, full of love and faith. Jayne was an inspiration to the Church and community. Her mother writes that: "She knew God was ready to share her problem from the very beginning."

I remember visiting her one Eastertide and she gave me a drawing she had done. It was of the crucifixion. Underneath she had written one word, 'Victory'. The victory of the Cross of Jesus. It was humbling and inspiring to see the victory of God's love in Jayne's personality over the suffering.

My visits to the home built up friendship with them all. Sometimes I called when the doctor was there and he would have tears in his eyes as he left.

Jayne became very perceptive about life as a whole. I can remember her saying to me, "I think God's favourite colours must be blue and green – the blue sky and the green of the trees and grass. Her favourite hymn was 'There is a green hill'. Based on a phrase from that she would say, "Bless Jesus because he's opened the gate of heaven for us."

Friendship of this quality draws people closer to God. It reminds me of the story of Margaret, a 15 year old girl in Kent who also showed remarkable faith whilst suffering from cancer. Her brother-in-law, J.D. Ross, found a deep faith in God through her friendship and her Christian faith. He wrote a book about her entitled 'Margaret' and in a broadcast interview had this to say:-
"She placed God, a real, vivid personality before me. Someone, who really knows our troubles and can help us with them. I like to think she introduced me to God."[18]

One of the great contributions that friendship makes to health and wholeness is the ministry of encouragement. St. Paul realised that truth in the help he received from 'our dear friend Luke the doctor'.

---

[18] This is my Story, William Purcell, Hodder, 1963. Reproduced by permission of David Higham Associates.

31

A young wife and mother in suffering writes of how everyone who suffers needs to be encouraged and how it helps the path through pain (Pathway Through Pain, Jane Grayshon, Hodder & Stoughton).

The early Christians were conscious of a deep sense of the spiritual bond that united them in friendship and faith, loyalty and love to the Lord and to one another. Jesus clearly sees friendship in terms of self-giving love.

"Greater love has no one than this that he lay down his life for his friends" (St. John 15 v.13 NIV). The Cross is the ultimate expression of Christian friendship for us.

"At its best, friendship is a love that is free from instinct, from jealousy, from the need to be needed and from all duties but those which love has freely assumed. Have we here found a natural love which is Love itself?"[19]

"We need friends when we are young to keep us from error, when we get old to tend upon us and to carry out those plans which we have not strength to execute ourselves, and in the prime of life to help us in noble deeds" *(Aristotle)*.

FRIENDSHIP

The writer of Ecclesiasticus says: 'A faithful friend is a strong defence; and he that has found such a one has found a treasure' (Chapter 6 v.14). Friendship is one of the greatest gifts of life, and a person who has no friends is much to be pitied. Our friends are very different from our relations: we choose our friends, but our family is given to us. Friends are the people we like to be with, and feel comfortable and 'at home' with. Our family and relations are there from the beginning, and we have to learn to live together with them. A person's friends say much about that person because, being chosen, we select friends who fit in with our likes and dislikes, our brand of humour, our type of personality, and so on. But all friendship has to be worked at: because we 'make' friends it is also very easy to lose friends unless we nurture and feed friendship.

Qualities which are enshrined in true friendship include loyalty, patience, and a sense of humour. We cannot always agree with other people, and it would be quite wrong to expect our friends to be a replica of ourselves in their views and personalities. Indeed,

---

[19] C.S. Lewis, Walter Hooper, Harper Collins p.372.

such an expectation would be boring and even dangerous. The fact that differences of opinion or likes and dislikes may occur is to be welcomed provided loyalty can persist. Differences often complement each other rather like cog wheels fitting together, and a friendship can often be richer for its variety of experience and the differing characters of the friends. However, no matter how much we may be irritated by some aspects of a friend's behaviour, our loyalty should ensure that we tolerate peculiarities sensibly and sensitively. It is often a mark of significant loyalty if we can accept honest criticism of our own shortcomings and irritations, and equally if we can give gentle criticism of our friend's weaknesses, without it leading to irretrievable breakdown. T.S. Eliot said that 'friendship should be more than biting time can sever', and such a constant quality can only be achieved by loyalty.

Together with loyalty must come patience: the ability to bite one's tongue at times, or to have a quiet chuckle to oneself, while accepting shortcomings and irritations, is essential. We have to remember that because true friendship is a mix of characters we need to accept patiently those aspects of our friends' qualities which we find hard to understand, just as of course they have to accept patiently our own peculiarities and eccentricities. If we can ally this patience with a sense of humour then much can be achieved gently, far more than if we try to ride roughshod over other people's views and feelings and personalities. To be able to laugh together at each other's peculiarities and failings must surely rank as one of the greatest tests and strengths of true friendship.

Equally, gentle banter, which avoids sarcasm or barbed criticism, can ease along a deepening and lasting friendship because it is a means of seeing ourselves as others see us, and being able to be amused by it. To be brave and honest enough to accept that, without offence, is a great gift. The deeper the friendship, the greater the two people's knowledge of each other becomes. If with that greater knowledge, warts and all, the friendship can develop and flourish, then it is friendship indeed. Friends who break up after differences of opinion, or deeper revelations of knowledge, are sadly not in the right mould for true friendship.

It is an interesting fact, but true, that one can have various different friends all of whom are one's own friends, but who quite possibly could not get on with each other as friends. This is because the complex nature of human character and personality has many facets, and, like the kaleidoscope, shines different patterns with different positions. It is a great privilege to have a variety of friends, and equally to be a friend of others who have many different friends too. In such a complexity of relationships, jealousy is one of the most dangerous weapons to threaten friendship.

A rich friendship, however, is one which can take on board such a complex pattern of relationships, knowing that the complexity itself will be the means by which the richness of our own total relationships will be enhanced. Inevitably, some friends are bound to be more 'special' than others, but I believe that it is quite feasible to have different 'special' friends for different 'special' circumstances. It would not be unreasonable, for example, for a friendship made special by a love of music to be different from a friendship with someone else made special by an enthusiasm for football. The common factor would be my love of both music and football, even though one friend could perhaps be tone deaf and the other bored by sport. It can sometimes make an interesting reflection on the immense variety and complexity of one's own character and personality to see what a motley combination can be randomly thrown together by a party, perhaps, or a wedding, or some other such get-together – all one's own friends but all quite different from each other.

According to the writer of the Book of Genesis, after God had created man in the beginning, He looked at the perfection of His creation and said: 'It is not good for man to be alone'. Although this statement is used by the writer to lead on to his description of God's creation of 'Woman', the statement itself is a basic fact of human existence. We are not meant to live as isolated beings: we only become truly human in relationship. The qualities of love and concern, of happiness and empathy, can only be properly expressed in relationship with other people. There are some particular horror stories of individuals who have so cocooned themselves in isolated independence that they have truly ceased to be human, and have developed peculiar traits of fear and greed and jealousy which have made them totally impossible to live with – sadly at times even impossible to live with themselves.

In friendship, there is the giving of a part of oneself to another person, which in certain circumstances may be costly. The most precious commodity most of us have is our time, and perhaps the most precious gift that we can each give to any friendship is our time. The ability to pick up the telephone and have a conversation with a friend without feeling that you are wasting their time is a priceless gift. The ability to receive a friend who has just 'popped round', and who will take you as they find you without any ceremony, is an equally priceless gift.

The ability to listen to a friend pouring out their frustrations and worries and anger, or equally their joys and success stories, without making them feel small and immature, is another priceless gift. The privilege of being asked for one's own opinion or advice in a friend's complicated decision making is a measure of respected friendship. The ability to tell another person personal confidences and to share personal problems, without the fear that such confidences and problems are likely to become common knowledge, must be one of the highest qualifications of sound friendship. Occasionally, of course, things go wrong. Either we make an error of judgement, or a friend lets us down, or we discover things about each other which lead each to question the desirability of continuing the friendship. Saying 'sorry' can often be one of the most difficult things to do, and yet can be one of the most significant signs of maturity (both in adults as well as children).

The highest gift of all, however, is forgiveness. While a row may occasionally clear the air, to be able to forgive a friend who for some reason has wronged us, is perhaps one of the greatest demands that friendship can make. Forgiveness is never a right; it is something given freely by another person, beyond what we have any right to expect. The forgiveness by one side however has to be matched by contrition on the other side. If either the forgiveness or the contrition are contrived and insincere, then the friendship is doomed. Forgiveness is the essence of all that Christianity understands about the relationship of God and man. The story of the Prodigal Son demonstrates the genuineness of the son's contrition and the genuineness of the father's forgiveness. If either side had been insincere, the relationship could not have been restored. The son had no right to expect forgiveness from his father, and the father had no reason to give it. The fact that it was given and received freely made the healing of the breach a genuine reconciliation. There are times when friendships can be painfully tested by a need for forgiveness to overcome a breakdown: if that can be achieved then often it can lead to an even more solid relationship.

So, is friendship only for saints? Are erring and weak humans unlikely to be able to achieve fulfilling friendships? I don't think so because, fortunately, we are all tarred with the same brush. It is not a case of the imperfect mixing with the perfect in most friendships – rather it is a case of two imperfect people making the best of a relationship. The emphasis has to be on 'making the best'. Friendship without some effort being put in by both sides is doomed. And if our friends are important enough to us, then we will ensure that we work constantly at contributing a fair share of effort into keeping the relationship healthy and flourishing. As Samuel Johnson said: 'A man should keep his friendship in constant repair.' If we can do that then we shall not only find fulfilment for ourselves, but we shall also have been the means of other people finding fulfilment too. 'A faithful friend is a medicine of life' (Ecclesiasticus chapter 6 v.16).

Alan Langton.

FRIENDSHIP OF JESUS
"Have we trials and temptations?
Is there trouble anywhere?
We should never be discouraged
Take it to the Lord in prayer
Can we find a friend so faithful
Who will all our sorrows share?
Jesus knows our every weakness
Take it to the Lord in prayer." *Joseph Scriven.*

"Friendship is the inexpressible comfort of feeling safe with a person: having neither to weigh up thoughts, nor measure words" *(George Eliot)*.

"No one can develop freely in this world and find a full life without feeling understood by at least one person" *(Dr. Paul Tournier).*

"There is a friend that sticketh closer than a brother" *(Proverbs 18 v.24).*

CHAPTER FIVE

THE MEDICAL/SPIRITUAL BALANCE

As someone who has been brought through mental illness by God working through the medical and spiritual balance, I am in no danger of belittling the importance of medical help.

There is always the temptation to try to limit our view of God's workings to our preconceived ideas. We are often tempted to forget that God is active outside Church life as well as inside it.

Some medics are sadly sceptical of the spiritual factors in health and wholeness: some Christians wrongly think there are total spiritual answers to complex health problems, and so mistakenly belittle the importance of medical help. This happens particularly in relation to mental health difficulties with sad pastoral consequences.

The patient who said, "We are prevented from dying, we are not helped to live," was emphasising the importance of the spiritual factors complementary to medicine.

The whole thrust of this book is the emphasis on the importance of the partnership of medical and spiritual in ministry amongst the sick. We need both because God is working through both.

The nature of this partnership is well put in the following statement of 1947 approved by the British Medical Association:-

"Medicine and the Church working together should encourage a dynamic philosophy of health which would enable every citizen to find a way of life based on moral principle and on a sound knowledge of the factors which promote health and well-being. Health is more than a physical problem, and the patient's attitude both to his illness and other problems is an important factor in his recovery and adjustment to life. Negative forces such as fear, resentment, jealousy and carelessness play no small part in the level of both personal and national health. For these reasons we welcome opportunities in the future for discussion and co-operation between qualified medical practitioners and all who have concern for the religious needs of their patients."[20]

---

[20] Quoted in Bp. Morris Maddocks 'The Christian Healing Ministry' S.P.C.K. P.164

Many illnesses are psychosomatic in their nature. A person's state of mind and circumstances in these situations has a profound effect on their physical health. For example a lot of worry and stress can produce inner disorders. There is increasing recognition of this in medical circles. Sir James Watt speaks of the importance of understanding the pre-clinical situation "in which stress, violence, bereavement, suppressed emotions, guilt, grief, or a sense of isolation are to be found" *(Journal of Religion and Medicine Dec. 1991)*.

In Shakespeare's 'Macbeth' a big challenge is put to a doctor:-
> "Canst thou not minister to a mind diseased.
> Pluck from the memory a rooted sorrow,
> Raze out the written troubles of the brain,
> And with some sweet oblivious antidote
> Cleanse the stuffed bosom of that perilous stuff
> Which weighs upon the heart?"

It will certainly need a multi-disciplinary team of care to begin to answer that searching question.

The achievement of medicine has been great in modern times. Many diseases have been largely conquered. Public health matters and preventive medicine generally have been considerably enhanced. There are far fewer deaths in childbirth. The discovery of penicillin by Alexander Fleming has paved the way for considerable success in treating infectious illness.

This success has in turn put tremendous pressure on the medical profession. The expectations of people are so high, the demands on health care are so great, especially with people living longer.

Medicine isn't just something done to us as if we were just a piece of chemistry. Patients need to participate positively so that we can assist in our health.

Dr. Michael Wilson saw that "health is being able to respond in a mature way to life as it is." [21] It is not just a case of personal individual health but of building a healthy society.

The Bible also sees the corporate nature of health as well as its individual aspect.

---

[21] The Hospital – 'A place of truth', University of Birmingham.

Such a realisation should guide public attitudes. As John Habgood reminds us the quality of a society should be judged by its approach towards its most vulnerable people.

I recall a sick elderly parishioner, living on his own, who was visited regularly by two young nieces. They assured him of their love for him and this was a great tonic to him. He commented to me, "Love is the best medicine of all."

An atmosphere of love is very necessary for bringing healing to those who are needing it, hence the great ideals of the nursing profession and the supreme emphasis on care. Some people have to be loved back to health. But in addition to this, a great love in the patient will strengthen his own will to live. Many have come through severe illnesses only because they have someone to love and to live for. To love and to know that one is loved are powerful means of healing.

An integral part of Christian healing must be to make the patient aware of God's love and so help him to be receptive. This is why all sacramental means of healing are so important.[22] It is this combination of truth and love which is so central to Christianity. It is focused in the Cross and Resurrection of Jesus in which through faith we can share.

It is the inspiration of all that is best in medicine whether that is recognised by its agents or not.

As that great pioneer surgeon Joseph Lister used to say "Love and truth are basic requirements for medicine." As he put it, "a warm and loving heart and truth in an earnest spirit."

In Roman times there was not much use of medication – the main treatments were physiotherapy, baths, diet and exercise. The Physician Celsus has recorded the importance of allaying anxiety and understanding the background to the illness with information from patients and relatives.

More recently a mechanistic approach to pastoral care has sometimes developed because of a failure by some to discern the essential spiritual nature of human beings.

Sir James Watt sees this danger, sees the reality of our spiritual nature, and so asks the challenging question "Is he (man) merely a biological entity equipped with conflicting emotions and surging hormones – a

---

[22] Douglas Webster, 'What is Spiritual Healing?' Highway Press p.17.

chemical factory programmed to respond to changing situations?"[23] Moreover people need not just physical betterment but meaning and purpose for life.

St. Paul realised this when he wrote, "Offer your bodies as living sacrifices, holy and pleasing to God – this is your spiritual act of worship. Do not conform any longer to the pattern of this world, but be transformed by the renewing of your mind. Then you will be able to test and approve what God's will is – his good, pleasing and perfect will." [24]

We must not belittle the vital role of medicine but we must face the fact that however advanced medicine becomes and however much prayer is offered, there will always in this earthly life be suffering. Some wrongly feel a sense of guilt about being ill, but physical and mental illness can come to anyone no matter how dedicated a Christian.

Some suffering is self-inflicted, some is inflicted by others, but much remains incapable of explanation. Such suffering is a mystery and there are no slick answers. It is also true that we don't have to be ill to experience suffering. Anyone who is caring and sensitive to the needs of others, suffers. That should mean all of us. It is only some of the selfish and uncaring who appear 'to get away with it', and we should never envy them. One day they will have to give an account to God. At the heart of our faith is the suffering Saviour, Jesus Christ. Here is the proof that God never sends suffering to us but comes to share it with us. The important role of the doctor in relieving suffering is well expressed in the Book of Ecclesiasticus:-

"Honour the doctor for his services, for the Lord created him. His skill comes from the most high. The Lord has created medicine from the earth, and a sensible man will not disparage this. The Lord has imparted knowledge to him, that by use of his marvels he may win praise: by using them the doctor relieves pain and from them the pharmacist makes up his mixture" *(from Chapter 38 NEB)*.

One of the problems that has weakened the trust between the medical and the spiritual sphere has been the upsurge in faith healing. This is not the authentic ministry of healing that God entrusts to his Church. The wrong assumptions behind faith healing are well exposed by Canon George Bennett in the words:-

---

[23] Journal of Religion and Medicine. Dec. 1991.
[24] Romans Chapter 12 v.1-2 NIV.

"Unfortunately we have much misunderstanding to overcome. So many people's minds have become confused by the faith healing image. A common mistake for example, is to think that you only need faith to be healed. This is quite wrong and can be cruelly so. To tell a sufferer that he must have faith is about as kind as telling a cripple to lift himself up by his own bootstraps. No, the whole onus of faith is on the Church and on those who try to bring help. It is Christ who heals, not faith" (from Wollaton Parish Magazine 'Link').

Faith healing also wrongly belittles the medical input, which has such an important role to perform. Health issues are increasingly putting a challenge to medicine as well as to the Church as the following article makes clear:-

The really unsolved problems of medicine.

Dr. Tony Short,
Clinical Skills Laboratory,
University of Nottingham Medical School.
(This article was drafted in 1999.)

We read much of the old enemies of health such as cancer and the challenge of new diseases such as AIDS. It is often made out that research into these will solve the remaining problems of medicine. But some are more difficult and fundamental than these. Learning the arts of a doctor has always been amongst the most challenging tasks that a young person could take up. In the modern era, when science and technology have given so much more power to diagnose and treat physical illness, one might consider the task to be now less formidable. Unhappily, the reverse is true.

Problems

We expect a lot of doctors. They rely a good deal on physical science and its methods so they need academic ability and grasp of science. Not all medical transactions are so defined – there is much respect within modern medicine and medical education for holistic medicine, attending to the whole patient. This means acknowledging the concerns of patients, the potential psychological dimension even of straightforwardly physical ailments, and the frequent association of ethical questions with medical tasks. Doctors in most fields of practice need to handle communications with patients across barriers of age, gender, ethnicity and culture.

The doctor's capacity for empathy, which we may define as entering into the patient's situation as he or she understands it, is also vital. This must extend to every patient, whether these barriers exist or not. Sometimes it must cross a greater barrier yet. How hard it is for the well and happy to empathise with the unhappy and distressed! Since we also expect our doctors to have equanimity, balance and calmness, willingness to take responsibility, honesty and a humane, kindly yet professionally detached interest in patients and their families, this is more like a formidable gulf than a mere barrier. We know there is much difficulty in this area, as we may judge by the presence throughout our society of an unfounded but pervasive sense of shame or stigma associated with mental illness, for which the medical profession cannot escape its share of blame.

All this raises vast problems for the selection and training of tomorrow's doctors. Yet there is more. What does it imply if we consider Man to be Body, Mind *and Spirit?* If the duties of a good doctor need to acknowledge this, in what way? If we find any answer to this, how can we train tomorrow's doctor in this domain? If we cannot offer training, can we pay attention to these issues in selection of medical school entrants? How, in particular, can we combine equity with spiritual and cultural diversity in a pluralistic society?

Today's medical students have overcome much competition for a place in the course, mainly by showing high academic ability in their teens. Many with good temperaments for the humane practice of medicine are being excluded, while some of those included may not really have them. They may, however, be quick enough of mind to be able to seem to have such qualities when writing an application or taking part in a short interview.

Thirty or forty years ago medicine was open to people of varied ability and academic interest. Today's entrants come exclusively from a scholarly fringe able to achieve grades A-star, A, B or better in three A-levels, of which two at least will be in physical sciences – or equivalent Scottish or Continental qualifications. During the same period there has been a marked expansion of medical knowledge. Doctors have coped with this by specialising more narrowly. Firstly, this makes it the more tempting for medical transactions to focus on the apparent condition or problem, again with the risk of losing sight of the whole patient. Secondly, the consequent eclipse in hospital practice of the general surgeon and even the general physician denies these as role models for those in general clinical training. This is a major loss, since contact with real doctors while they are treating real patients is the only known way of learning medicine, however much books, lectures and laboratories help us to learn *about* medicine. Fortunately, general clinical experience has become available in the community by greatly expanding the teaching role of family doctors and their patients.

Increased flows of health-related information in the modern media could, one might hope, have produced improvements in lifestyle and better health, with reduction in the economic burden of healthcare and welfare. It has, however, not yet passed beyond the raising of anxiety, demand for more services, and irrational expectations of what health services can deliver. Urban life in the twenty-first century seems likely to be at least as stressful as it ever was, while smaller proportions of our community enjoy the solaces of religion or even the ethical basis of a secure upbringing or a settled family life. These factors tend both to increase the inner needs of patients and to impair the inner resources of their doctors.

Responses

We have to admit we have no robust means either to improve the qualities needed by a young potential carer or validly to select for them. How in all these circumstances can we bring it about that a school-leaver becomes in a few short years someone who can care, and give care without stint over time?

The General Medical Council (GMC) has helped by spelling out in recent publications such as *Tomorrow's Doctors* (1993) and *The New Doctor* (1997) what medical undergraduate courses should provide, and what basic standards should be insisted upon. These stimuli have provoked extensive modification of every undergraduate medical course in Britain. Better emphasis is now being given to the humane and holistic in medicine. For example, the cultivation of good communication skills has become a universally recognised function of core undergraduate training. Similarly, no course now wholly lacks explicit instruction in and discussion of the major ethical issues in medicine. *Tomorrow's Doctors* also gave medical schools a clear invitation to identify a carefully edited compulsory core of knowledge, skills and attitudes needed by any entrant to the profession. To this core, we are encouraged to add variety through optional Special Study Modules (SSMs) of which the student would select a few. Every medical school has now developed an extensive catalogue of SSMs, of which more is said in the final paragraph.

Accountability in publicly funded higher education has increased through the Quality Assurance process commissioned by the Higher Education Funding Councils. While the paperwork and inspections by which this is enforced are proving to be an unwelcome increase in workload for university staff, the raising of standards (particularly of educational audit and of student welfare provision) is already apparent. There is much more dissemination of good ideas in higher education and assessment, while complacency and arrogance, that were common, have been seriously dented.

Efforts have been made to provide better structures, career guidance and assessment processes for general clinical training, for specialty training and for continuing medical education. These will take some years to bed down and bear full fruit, but many of these are such improvements on past practice as to be certain to yield net benefit. The GMC has also developed its roles in recognising and organising support for sick doctors, and in dealing with poor professional performance in doctors. Not only will those individual doctors and their patients benefit, but the existence of these processes will militate against professional complacency more effectively than did the GMC's past actions solely against crime and malpractice.

What remains to be done?
The ability to care comes mainly from early upbringing, character and belief. It is generous, consistent, never patronises, never judges (see *1 Corinthians* chapter 13 verse 4). Since we cannot undertake to change character in the undergraduate course, we need better means of choosing our future doctors, ways that will reliably identify those with the capacities for compassion, empathy and equanimity we need.

Patients, nurses and family doctors are probably better placed than anyone to recognise potential doctors and nurses in their own community. At present the only personal assessment on the UCAS application form is that of a senior secondary school teacher. Valuable as this is, it does not seem to be enough to ensure that compassion and social maturity rank at least equally with academic ability. Perhaps we should expect community sponsors willing to write about and also to be interviewed about an applicant for medical training?

We should more often encourage and facilitate the broadening of the experience of applicants before medical school entry, so long as the way the year or two after leaving school is spent does not undermine the ability to study. We should also give far better consideration to and support for mature students who wish to enter medicine. Not only will they have grown up (which some school leavers plainly have not), but there will be more proof of their settled values and character, and more evidence of their steadiness. It is a false economy that denies mature entrants even the exiguous financial support available to school leavers.

Admission interviews need to be longer, supplemented with other forms of evaluation, and involve, to a greater extent than at present, experienced members of the general community in its cultural diversity. This would undoubtedly increase the expense and difficulty of the admission process, but the costs of medical education are so high, and the further costs attributable to the actions of students or doctors who fail are higher yet.

One aspect that seems vital, to which at present we can give only scant regard, is assessment of the origin, quality and stability of the belief system of the applicant. At present, all we can achieve is a brief enquiry about the applicant's reasons for choosing medicine as a career, and our willingness to accept a little experience of care of the young or elderly as evidence that the applicant knows what might be involved in a caring career. It would be good to have evidence that applicants habitually respect the interests of other people such as parents and siblings, have coped with hardship over a longer period than a camping trip, and retain an astonishment at the world about them that has not been sated by a chemistry A-level. If applicants were believing Christians or religious Jews, I would like to hear them read out and discuss Psalm 139. There must be similar passages in the other sacred writings. It would be good to have some such ground of deep discussion with humanists. What would agnostics, atheists and secularists propose? In the present state of law and custom, such enquiry would be generally regarded with alarm, embarrassment or disdain. Must this continue to be a "no-go area" for medical schools?

Special Study Modules (SSMs) on clinical topics are very interesting to students, and of particular value as sources of career guidance. Some schools go further and offer SSMs on topics in humanities, history, philosophy or literature. These can widen and deepen the sympathies of medical students, and nourish and steady their spirits by offering a little leisure to read more widely, to reflect on great issues, and to spend some time with people outside medicine. This is one of few developments that seems to offer progress towards solution of these deepest and most puzzling unsolved problems of medical education and doctoring.

The views in this article are those of the author personally.
Dr. Tony Short

The most important healing is inner healing – healing in our personalities – this we can experience even if we are suffering from an illness that has no physical cure. Our final healing awaits us beyond death when we are given our resurrection body in Christ, a spiritual body which does not suffer in any way, and when as the Bible movingly puts it, "God wipes away all tears from our eyes" (Revelation 21 v.4).

CHAPTER SIX

THE BIBLE'S PRESCRIPTION

It's not so much what we make of the Bible but what the Bible makes of us. It can transform our whole way of life if we will let it. It proclaims that the key to life is in self-giving love inspired by God (see for example, Isaiah chapter 53 and St. John chapter 3 verse 16).

Many with little or no faith to start with have come to experience God's life-giving presence through its pages and so have journeyed to wholeness.

A classical scholar did a translation of the Four Gospels for Penguin Books many years ago. It was a profound spiritual experience for him. He speaks in the Introduction to his translation, of the Gospels as being the Magna Carta of the human spirit. He writes of our need to devote more enthusiasm to them. His sense of the freshness of it all gave him the feeling that Christianity had only just begun. This is the journey to wholeness.

There is a difference between being physically cured and being whole. An eminent doctor, Sir John Stallworthy, speaks of the distinction there is between healing just in the sense of physical betterment and healing in our personality. Sir John and the Bible would understand the latter as wholeness. He points out that whilst all ten lepers in Luke chapter 17 were physically cured, there was one of them who had a deeper healing. The one who went back to Jesus to say thank you clearly had an inner transformation also. He was made whole. There is a difference between being physically cured and being whole. In an address in Oxford, Sir John said the narrative in Luke and Luke's account of the woman with the uterine bleeding illustrates the truth that "some people are more at peace, more a whole personality with incurable disease than others are whose sickness has been replaced by physical fitness."[25]

The name Jesus is the Greek form of the Hebrew Joshua. It means Saviour. It derives from a Hebrew root that means 'to be spacious'. Donald Coggan writes that the Bible shows that the wholeness of humanity is freedom from all that hinders fullness of life. It implies integration of body, mind and spirit (see Christian Priorities p.110-111 Lutterworth).

---

[25] Sermons from St. Aldate's, edited by Keith de Berry – Hodder & Stoughton p.106.

Jesus rejects the view of much of the Old Testament that suffering is a result of sin. Much suffering clearly is not. "Jesus is soter, which means both 'Saviour' and 'Healer'. Jesus denies the crude view that all illness is retribution, nevertheless maintains that his power over disease is evidence of his power to forgive sin."[26]

"When Tyndale makes Christ to say to Zacchaeus, 'This day is health come to thy house' his translation spoke deeper than he knew and made luminous the deep interest of Christ for true health is impossible apart from God."[27] So a vital ingredient of the mission of Jesus for the world's redemption is this emphasis on people's need for wholeness.

Jesus in the gospels clearly showed that illness was something to be fought. He was never resigned to it – nor should we be so. He also did not just concentrate on the physical nature of the problem. He saw behind the symptoms to the underlying causes, including the emotional, moral and spiritual nature of the difficulty. For instance in Mark chapter 2, as well as the sick person's paralysis there was inward need to be met, including his need for forgiveness for some fault.

Jesus made clear that it was wrong to say there was a straight co-relation between sin and sickness. The book of Job had been a protest against this too. Some illness obviously has its roots in moral failure. Much illness however comes to lovely dedicated people. Also always remember we follow a suffering Saviour. There is a mysterious union between love and suffering. The Cross of Jesus is the meeting place between Divine love and human suffering.

In St. John chapter 9 Jesus says it was neither that the man had sinned nor his parents that he was born blind. God through the Cross shares suffering with us. The prophecy in Isaiah 53 of the suffering Saviour is fulfilled in Jesus. "Surely he took up our infirmities and carried out sorrows" (NIV). The Bible sees the way God works through both the medical and spiritual aspects. For example in Psalm 147 we read "He heals the broken-hearted and binds up their wounds" (NIV).

The Gospels show how Jesus used medication in those days in His work of health and wholeness. The spittle of a holy person was believed to have therapeutic properties. In Mark chapter 7 he uses that as He touches the tongue of a deaf man. In John chapter 9 He used His saliva to make some mud and put it on that patient's eyes.

The Bible sees the sickness of the human condition and our need for health and wholeness. Jesus in his sermon at Nazareth recorded in Luke

---

[26] Alan Richardson, Theological Word Book of the Bible p.103 S.C.M.
[27] Donald Coggan, 'Convictions' p.272-3 Hodder reproduced by permission of Hodder & Stoughton Ltd.

chapter 4 quotes the passage in Isaiah 61 – good news for the poor, freedom for those in the prison house of fear, release for those suffering from various forms of oppression, and healing for the broken-hearted. So Jesus sees the wide-range of sickness and handicap that needs healing – in political and social life as well as personal life. Isaiah in chapter 1 also sees the sickness of society:

"Your whole head is sick, and your whole heart diseased."

"From the sole of your feet to the top of your head, no single part is sound." *(J.B. Phillips, translation)*

We all need the healing touch of Christ. That is a vital point that the Bible makes clear.

As Douglas Webster puts it, "We must never strike the attitude of being whole men and women moving with pity among the sick. To the end of our days we are infected men, in the process of being healed and sanctified by the Lord Jesus, but never completely whole because never completely his. We can only offer Christ our spoiled and bungled lives."[28]

The sermon at Nazareth exposes the sickness of racial prejudice which still stains much of life. Jesus seeks to heal this, quoting examples of the healings exercised through Elijah and Elisha, showing God's healing reaching out to non-Jews, the widow at Zarephath and Naaman the Syrian. God's health and wholeness ministry is intended for all. Nor is it an isolated thing. It should be in the context of teaching and pastoral care.

Rev. Barrie Cooke writes:

Preach insubstantial sermons and we produce insubstantial Christians. Share the truth of holy Scripture and we create a people who are motivated and strong. Our minds as well as our bodies clamour to be fed. What we give them 'to eat' has a profound effect on our state of health.

When Jesus made his debut in Galilee he quoted the Scriptures: 'The Spirit of the Lord is on me, because he has anointed me to preach good news to the poor. He has sent me to proclaim freedom for the prisoners and recovery of sight for the blind, to release the oppressed, to proclaim the year of the Lord's favour' (NIV). When we preach that gospel we surely make the ministry of preaching a ministry of healing. To put it another way: preaching should sometimes be like a surgeon's scalpel, cutting to heal; at other times it applies the ointment of the gospel to wounds that need treatment.

---

[28] P.8 The Healing Christ, Highway Press

May I make a plea that we explore with our people the healing miracles of Jesus. Not turning them into parables as is the wont of some of us, but demonstrating their significance in the context of our own need for health.

I would like to see our churches truly becoming healing communities. I would love to see prayer chains, healing services, intercessory groups in every church's programme, but we mustn't think that setting up such services makes a church into a healing community. If we would become a healing community we must above all attend to relationships within the local congregation (Barrie Cooke in an article in the Methodist Health and Healing Magazine 1992).

Luke describes the way in which God's ministry of health and wholeness is intended for all. "When the sun was setting, the people brought to Jesus all who had various kinds of sickness and laying his hands on each one, he healed them" (Luke 4 v.40 NIV).

"The love of Christ, the healing action of Christ, the compassion of Christ are 'with undistinguishing regard'. No means test; no morality test; no religious test. The sheer outgoing love of Jesus, the love of God, is the motivating power."[29] "At daybreak Jesus went out to a solitary place" (Luke 4 v.42 NIV). Jesus needed to withdraw so that he could go back into his caring work with strength renewed. Here is a key principle for all carers. We need to charge our spiritual batteries to be most effective and rightly motivated in caring work. Prayer is the secret of it all.

HEALING AND THE BIBLE

They walked out of the chapel together and approached me as I stood by the door. It was January 25 at The Old Rectory, Crowhurst, and the Feast of the Conversion of St. Paul. I had been speaking about conversion in Christian experience, and of the change God brings about in the lives of those made new in Christ Jesus, and how this is the work of the Holy Spirit. 'Do you really mean that God can be as real to us as that, and in such a personal way?' they asked. I replied that this is so. 'We have been going to church for years, but never heard about this before,' they said. We went into the small chapel which also served as a vestry, and sat talking. The result was that before long the three of us were kneeling at the altar rail, where they invited Christ into their own lives.

---

[29] Douglas Webster, The Healing Christ p.23-4, Highway Press.

This followed a direct application of a Bible passage, as it came home to them. Through hearing the Word, Christ became real in their own experience. Some weeks later they wrote to say what a vast difference this meeting with the Lord had brought about. 'Whereas there used to be only two of us, now there is always three of us', was the way she put it. They had many problems, and this was the reason for their coming to us in the first place. It would not be true to say that all those problems were resolved there and then. This rarely, if ever, happens. But it makes all the difference when Another walks with you.

On other occasions someone would approach us as they left the chapel after a service and say 'I had intended to come and see one of you for counselling, but my problem seems to have been answered in the chapel.'

When we speak of the Christian healing ministry, we usually think in terms of the laying-on-of-hands, anointing, counselling, and the Eucharist. And of course, all these ministries have a vital place. They are God-given and Bible-based and important ways through which the Spirit ministers to us. Yet sometimes it seems that God cuts through to the heart of the problem by some penetrating word from the Scriptures.

We need not be surprised at this. After all, the Bible says that 'the word of God is living and active, sharper than any two-edged sword' (Hebrews chapter 4 v.12), and that 'all Scripture is inspired by God, and is profitable' (2 Timothy chapter 3 v.16). We may therefore expect the Bible to have a direct part in the healing of lives and relationships.

The Word of God is indeed active; active in **converting.** I related the instance of the couple who said 'now there is always three of us'. In one of my parishes a family came to know Christ because the mother came to church and sat reading an old, very Victorian style of text in gothic letters, over the chancel arch: 'Christ Jesus came into the world to save sinners.' The words went to her heart, and before long her family was involved. Previously, when we had re-decorated the church, I had wanted that text removed. How glad I am the PCC overruled me!

The Word of God is active in **assuring.** It assures me that I can be what I am, without need of pretence. Read the Psalms, and see how 'natural' the writers are. They don't delude themselves or deny what is happening. They don't play games with God, or try to fool themselves. See, for example, Psalm 77 v.1-10 or Psalm 130, 'out of the deep'. It allows me to be angry, even with God – See Jeremiah chapter 20 v.7. It allows me to cry (Psalm 42 v.1-3). It is all right to be 'carried' (Isaiah chapter 63 v.9). Healing can begin to flow when I cease keeping up some false façade, and begin 'being myself'.

Finally the Word is active in **hope.** See Psalm 130 again, particularly verses 5 onwards (my version is the R.S.V.) 'I wait.... I hope...He will.' Assurance and hope are vital elements in healing.

Perhaps the last word could go to the old collect for Bible Sunday, (Second in Advent):'Grant that we may hear them (the Scriptures), read, mark, learn, and inwardly digest them, that by patience and comfort (strengthening) of your holy word, we may ever hold fast the blessed hope of everlasting life in our Saviour, Jesus Christ.'

David Howell.

Although Jesus makes clear that there is no straight co-relation between sin and sickness, obviously in some health problems the ingredient of forgiveness is important – the need for forgiveness which we should recognise and accept, and also the readiness to extend forgiveness to those who have wronged us, not least for our own peace of mind.

"Anyone who is preaching forgiveness and practising it in the whole network of life's complicated relationships with all their irritations and unconscious resentments, is exercising a ministry of healing all Christians are charged with."[30]

The Cross is Christ's supreme act of healing. The Cross heals at the deepest level wounded relationships between us and God, and so between us and other people. This is the ministry of reconciliation of which St. Paul speaks.

"Therefore, if anyone is in Christ, he is a new creation: the old has gone, the new has come! All this is from God, who reconciled us to himself through Christ and gave us the ministry of reconciliation" (2 Corinthians 5 v.17-18 NIV).

God is assisted in his healing of society by people who are in the process of being healed. A good example of this is Gordon Wilson in Northern Ireland. His work for healing there has been outstanding after the tragic death of his daughter, Marie, through terrorism.

---

[30] Douglas Webster – Ibid.

Here are his words:-

"I believe I do my best in human terms to show forgiveness, but the last word rests with God and those who seek his forgiveness will need to repent.[31] I'm not going to add to the hatreds by talking about bitterness or revenge. I'll go on praying for all of them and leave the rest to God. That's the only way I can handle it, and still live with myself."[32]

---

[31] Marie p.93 Marshall Pickering: Harper Collins
[32] Ibid. p.94.

CHAPTER SEVEN

MUSIC THERAPY

No one can doubt the mental and emotional effects of music. For example it was found during World War 2 that cheerful music in our factories boosted production. Suitable music over the centuries has been found to calm people and give peace of mind. Shakespeare was clearly aware of this. Think for example of a speech in 'The Merchant of Venice' where the lines come:-

> "How sweet the moonlight sleeps upon this bank
> Here will we sit, and let the sounds of music
> Creep in our ears: soft stillness and the night
> Become the touches of sweet harmony…..
> Such harmony is in immortal souls."

J.S. Bach wrote that, "All music should have no other end and aim than the glory of God and the recreation of the soul."

Vaughan Williams was a composer who spoke to the spiritual nature of people. In 1920 he wrote an essay in which he said, "The object of all art is to obtain a partial revelation of that which is beyond human senses and human faculties – of that which is in fact spiritual." Beethoven was very keen on the freedom of the human spirit and in his 'Missa Solemnis' wrote over part of the score 'A prayer for inner and outer peace.'

Music therapy is much used nowadays in helping the ill or the handicapped to express themselves.

"Music therapy first began with the structured use of music and of specific techniques to help people who are ill or handicapped. It is now also being used successfully in promoting health for people who are stressed, anxious or lonely, or with people who want to overcome communication problems, or to enhance their creativity."[33]

We know that music was used as a therapy by early civilisation, Egyptians, Persians, Greeks, etc.

Music was clearly a powerful factor in the life of the Jews as the Old Testament records. The Psalms are expression of the heights and depths of spiritual feeling.

The Psalmist highlighted the talents of the musicians in expressing praise and gratitude to God – a big factor in inner healing.

---

[33] Sarah Caird, Journal of Institute of Religion and Medicine, April 1987.

Here is a quote from Psalm 150:-
>"Praise the Lord.
>Praise him with the sound of the trumpet,
>Praise him with the harp and lyre
>Praise him with tambourine and dancing
>Praise him with the strings and flute
>Praise him with the clash of symbols,
>Praise him with resounding symbols...."

>"Praise is inner health made audible.
>Lord teach us to adore." (C.S. Lewis).

In 1 Samuel 16 verses 14-23 there is described how David by music set out to heal Saul's obsessive depression.

In the New Testament St. Paul urges his readers to express their gratitude in "psalms, hymns and spiritual songs" (Colossians 3 verse 17).

Many people sick in mind or body find that music draws out spiritual strength to help to cleanse the emotions and relieve distress, anxiety and pain.

The great philosopher, Aristotle, felt that music is the most 'moral' of all the arts, influencing character most directly.

Music is used in psychotherapy helping to make a bridge between reality and the unreal world in the patient's mind. It can help to bring to the surface some of the things hidden in the subconscious mind of the sufferer.

Nottingham pianist Philip Humphreys who has used music to help the physically and mentally handicapped writes as follows:-

MUSIC AND THE CARE OF THOSE WITH LEARNING DIFFICULTIES

In considering the important part which music may play in the care of those with learning difficulties (both adults and children), four aspects seem particularly important.

Firstly, the language of music is obviously both immediate and universal. When other avenues of communication – words, ideas, indeed all 'intellectual' activity - are barred, music may yet be able to reach the human spirit and bring emotional richness.

Secondly, I have so often found in my work that rhythm (particularly powerful and exaggerated rhythms) brings a kind of pleasure, even release to those who are disabled by learning difficulties. This experience may, of course, be further enhanced by the use of simple percussion instruments thus inducing further vibration and rhythmic impulse. I experienced a rather bizarre but nonetheless moving illustration of this effect when I was regularly playing the piano to a group of residents in a unit for those with learning difficulties. One of the young women on hearing a particularly rhythmic piece would 'come alive' and more disturbingly immediately begin to remove all her clothing!

Thirdly, assuming that routine and repetition are important to those who are disabled in this way I discovered that songs repeated often enough would become a point of recognition and so of great pleasure – in the end my friends 'owned' the songs.   The introduction of a well-known song would elicit a tremendous sense of welcome just as if a long-lost friend had entered the room.   I imagine that this recognition was playing some small part in the deepening of personal security and well-being.   ("John" for instance would insist on 'Jingle Bells' at all times and during all seasons!   Imagine singing the song on a blazing hot June afternoon!)

Lastly, I would point to that important sense of community which music-making of all kinds brings to our lives.   Whether it was by playing percussion instruments, singing or dancing.   I'm convinced that a sense of belonging together was being developed through our musical activity.   That musical activity was in fact constantly drawing us towards one another, and enriching lives which could well have been profoundly isolated.   Philip N. Humphreys.

Haydn saw his Oratorio 'The Creation' very much as a spiritual work. When there was applause at the words 'Let there be light' he is said to have pointed his hands in a heavenward direction and shouted out "It comes from there!" He felt that his regular prayers during the composition of the work were a crucial factor. "Everyday I fell to my knees and prayed God to grant me strength for a happy completion of this work." He saw prayer as a regular inspiration in his compositions. Indeed his humility brought him the therapy of much love from the public in his day.

The composer Beethoven found great support in spiritual values during the distressing adversity of his increasing deafness. He felt that God shared with him the unfairness of it all. He had an untraditional faith in God but a very personal faith.

Beethoven wrote, "Therefore, calmly will I submit myself to all inconsistency, and will place all my confidence in your eternal goodness, O God. My soul, shall rejoice in Thee, immutable Being. Be my rock, my light, forever my trust!"[34] His deafness had deprived him of friendship but he said that he felt God near to him. A favourite Bible text of his was the saying of Jesus to us, "Love one another."

---

[34] Quoted by Maynard Solomon, Beethoven Essays: Cambridge, Harvard University Press, 1988, p.223.

Many composers poured out their creative work with heightened sensitivity through the traumas of suffering. Many of their great works were not appreciated at the time.

J.S. Bach's music was apparently little known outside the area in which he worked till some years after his death. However, they still persevered. Sometimes their efforts were not really truly interpreted. Handel felt he saw a vision of God during his inspired writing of the 'Messiah'. When he was congratulated on its first London performance one person said to him that he'd provided excellent entertainment. He replied that it was not his purpose to entertain people but to make them better. Like John the author of Revelation he had seen 'through the door opening into heaven' (Revelation 4 verse 1).

Mozart produced an amazing output of spiritual music in his short life on earth, dying at the young age of 35. He too faced much suffering including poverty, but he believed firmly that the issues of life and death are in the hands of God – not man. "For this blessing I daily thank my Creator and wish it from my heart for all my fellow men."[35]

Amongst the modern composers, Stravinsky felt that music is a form of communion with God and his fellow human beings.

One of the most loved conductors of modern times is Malcolm Sargent. He struggled with a tubercular abscess and then later with cancer. His only daughter, Pamela, died of polio when young. As he sat for many hours by his daughter's bedside he was at work orchestrating the accompaniment to Brahms' 'Four Serious Songs'. These were texts from the Bible, from the pessimism of the Book of Ecclesiastes to St. Paul's great statement about the three lasting qualities of faith, hope and love.

As he lay dying he said he had loved this life so much that he was sure he would love death even more. As he put it, "When I go into the next world I shall not feel a stranger. As a child taken from the left breast cries only to find consolation in the right breast, so shall it be when we pass from life to death, from life to life."[36]

Many people battle with fear of death but a sure trust in God's love helped him to overcome such fear. He was ready to let go and to hand over to God as we need to do.

Commenting on 2 Chronicles chapter 5 v.13, J.S. Bach wrote, "When there's devotional music, God is always at hand with his gracious presence."

The Christian Church has always been a singing Church, reflecting the joy of Christ's Resurrection and the compassion of His Cross.

---

[35] Quoted by W.J. Turner in Mozart the Man and His work Westport, Conn. Greenwood 1938.

[36] Malcolm Sargent by Charles Reid, p.4, Hodder and Stoughton.

This is a therapy in itself. One of the greatest hymns is 'When I survey the wondrous Cross' by Isaac Watts. The therapy of God's amazing love is wonderfully expressed in it, especially the last verse.

Herewith acknowledgement of the help given me by 'Spiritual Lives of the Great Composers' by Patrick Kavanaugh. Zondervan (Harper Collins).

CHAPTER EIGHT
THE CUP OF HEALING

Nowhere is the meaning of the Holy Communion in all its simplicity more profoundly summed up than in the words attributed to Queen Elizabeth I:

> "Christ's were the words that spake it,
> He took the bread and brake it,
> And what that word doth make it
> That I believe and take it."

To see Holy Communion in that light is to avoid all the needless controversies about its interpretation that have disfigured Church history, and still sadly cause division. It emphasises the action of God through this Sacrament, and of our response of trust in His effectual working. It is to journey towards wholeness.

We live by faith in God, and it is therefore a reassuring help that God has given us the sacrament of Holy Communion. Here is something that we can touch – through which the spiritual strength of God flows into us. This is particularly valuable to those burdened in mind. An early Christian described it as 'the medicine of immortality', and another described it as 'healing food'.

Whatever our feelings, whether of elation or adversity, provided we receive in love, repentance and faith, God reaches into us. Here is a visual aid emphasising the dependability of God's love for us.

The Last Supper when Jesus initiated it for us has proved to be the first of many suppers. Here are visible tokens of Christ's Cross and Resurrection – healing spiritual food. As the words of administration put it, "preserve thy body and soul unto everlasting life." J.B. Phillips writes that Holy Communion will always be to those who love and believe an "APPOINTMENT WITH GOD."[37]

"The sheer stupendous quality of the love of God which this ever repeated action has drawn from obscure Christian multitudes through the centuries is in itself an overwhelming thought."[38]

"The reality of our communion with Christ and in Him with one another is the increase of love in our hearts" (William Temple).

---

[37] Appointment with God, p.74 –75, J.B. Phillips, Epworth.

[38] Gregory Dix, The Shape of the Liturgy, p.745, Dacre Press.

Often health is damaged by bitterness and resentment. Holy Communion provides a great opportunity to hand all this over to God. This handing over is difficult but it needs to be done.

The Holy Communion conveys the forgiving power of the Cross to us. This is cleansing and liberating. It is like a poultice on a wound drawing out the pus. "Repentance, sorrow for sin, the frank admission of failure, a deep desire for forgiveness: these necessities for healthy living are focused in every celebration of the Eucharist. In this sense, among others, it is a health-giving exercise."[39]

Within the Eucharist we have a special opportunity to repent of our sins and to be assured of God's forgiveness. It sometimes also needs the skilled help of a counsellor or psychotherapist to deal with our irrational guilt.

Another healthy feature of the Holy Communion is the way in which it presents us with the timeless presence of Christ and so helps the bereaved. This enables us in grief to say in prayers at Communion to Christ the things that we wish we'd said to our loved ones on earth.

As Bishop Morris Maddocks has written it was helpful to link the comfortable words with the Sacrament, "Come unto me all you that are heavy laden and I will refresh you."[40]

Holy Communion also provides a wonderful opportunity for us to express our gratitude for life's blessings. This sense of thankfulness is a vital ingredient in health and wholeness.

"By prayer and petition with thanksgiving present your requests to God. And the peace of God which passes all understanding will guard your hearts and minds in Christ Jesus ....whatever is true, whatever is noble, whatever is right, whatever is pure, whatever is lovely, whatever is admirable – if anything is excellent or praiseworthy – think about such things" (Philippians 4 v.7-8 NIV).

All this gives us a sense of vision which helps us along the journey to wholeness. We are enabled to see life not just as it really is, but as it can be when it comes under the transforming influence of God.

We are encouraged to offer more and more of ourselves to God in Holy Communion, including our broken-ness. The broken bread and poured out wine are such a powerful visual symbol of our wounded Healer, Jesus. As a modern hymn puts it:-

> "For the sacramental breaking,
> For the honour of partaking,

---

[39] Healing Experiences, Howard Booth B.R.F. p.57.

[40] Bp. Morris Maddocks. The Christian Healing Ministry S.P.C.K. p.115.

For your life our lives re-making,
Young and old we praise your name."
(Fred Kaan, Hymns Ancient & Modern New Standard. Hymns Ancient & Modern Ltd.)

This self-giving love is at the heart of the meaning of life. The more we give of ourselves to God and to the service of people, the more we become fulfilled and move towards wholeness. This way produces inner healing no matter what our physical or mental afflictions. The fundamental clash in life is between self-giving love and self-assertion. This caused the crucifixion of Jesus. His way of self-giving love triumphed and so set the pattern and inspiration for our self-giving love.

Holy Communion visibly portrays and conveys the Cross and the Resurrection of Jesus, and so assists our journey to wholeness.

"He who gave himself on Calvary gives Calvary to us, that we may give back our all to him.... the reality of our offering is tested by the genuineness of our care for our neighbour, and our will to serve the community with the love that flows from Christ crucified."[41]

"For centuries it has been the instinct of the Church to pray for the sick at the Sunday Eucharist. And not only for sick individuals, but also for the church and the world – also sick! It should be the intention of celebrant and worshippers to bring all for whom they pray under the broken body and shed blood of Christ, and under the power and authority of His Cross from which all healing flows, for 'by His wounds you have been healed.'"[42]

Commenting on Christ's words 'Do this in remembrance of me,' Gonville Ffrench-Beytough writes, "What Jesus is saying is 'Do this for the recalling of me into the **present.**' This is his means, instituted by himself, which we can use at our volition to bring him, simply because he loves us, 'out of the everywhere' into 'here' and into the 'now', into the lives which we are leading, into our situation, and indeed, when we receive him in Communion into ourselves, for the feeding of our souls and bodies."[43]

The mutual fellowship life of true Christian community helps to lessen loneliness and is a healing factor. "Christian fellowship in the Holy Communion is expressed today in the sharing of the Peace, a revival of an ancient custom. The whole action of the service demonstrates our oneness with Christ and each other.'"[44]

---

[41] Michael Ramsey, Introducing the Christian Faith, p.74 S.C.M. Press.

[42] David Howell p.11 Healing and Holy Communion, A Crowhurst occasional paper.

[43] Encountering Light p.59, Collins.

[44] David Howell ibid. p.9.

"The nearer we come to the Cross, the nearer we come to one another. This is the mystery of Christian community" (Moltmann).

We come to communion at Christ's invitation to receive His healing inner strength.

> "Lord this is Bread of heaven, Bread of life,
> That whoso eateth: never shall hunger more,
> And this the cup of pardon, healing, gladness, strength,
> That whoso drinketh, thirsteth not again.
> So may we come, O Lord, to thy Table,
> Lord Jesus, come to us."

From a prayer in 'A Procession of Passion Prayers.' (E. Milner-White S.P.C.K. reproduced by kind permission of the Friends of York Minster).

John Wardle writes:

Holy Communion, Healing and Wholeness

For Christians Holy Communion (The Eucharist) is the most important act of worship of the Church. This is because Jesus himself commanded his disciples to remember him in the 'breaking of bread'. The word 'eucharistic' comes from the Greek word 'to give thanks'. We give thanks to God the Father for his coming into the world in Jesus, re-calling the passion, death and resurrection of Jesus and realising his presence with his people in and through his Holy Spirit.

David Howell, formerly chaplain at The Old Rectory, Crowhurst, writes about Holy Communion as 'The Meeting Point', inspired by a painting with that title that he had noticed in a church vestry. He points to three 'meeting points' within the liturgy; as we look at each of these in turn we see the intrinsic healing and wholeness which Christ brings. (David Howell, Healing and Holy Communion, A Crowhurst Occasional Paper p.2.)

First, 'The Meeting Point with Christ'. St. Paul's account of the Last Supper records our Lord's words in detail:-

"For I received from the Lord what I also passed on to you: the Lord Jesus, on the night he was betrayed, took bread, and when he had given thanks, he broke it and said, 'This is my body which is for you: do this in remembrance of me.' In the same way, after supper he took the cup, saying, 'This cup is the new covenant in my blood; do this, whenever you drink it, in remembrance of me.' " (1 Corinthians 11 v.23-25 NIV).

St. Paul also writes in the previous chapter:-

"Is not the cup of thanksgiving for which we give thanks a participation in the blood of Christ? And is not the bread which we break a participation in the body of Christ? Because there is one loaf, we, who are many, are one body, for we all partake of the one loaf" (1 Corinthians 10 v.16-17 NIV).

Our attention is drawn here to 'remembrance' and 'communion' ('sharing' NRSV). The Holy Communion service is first an occasion for remembering Jesus. Bringing to mind God's saving work when Jesus offered himself 'a full, perfect and sufficient sacrifice, oblation and satisfaction for the sins of the whole world' (in the words of the Book of Common Prayer) we receive the benefits of his Passion. As we say the confession and receive the absolution we are allowing God to remove obstacles which stand in the way of our wholeness, our sin and lack of forgiveness. We are reconciled to God and to one another and through the repair of those relationships comes healing.

Later in the service we declare, *'The Lord is here, His Spirit is with us.'* There is a real meeting with Christ as he draws us again into a partnership of love (Communion, 'koinonia' in Greek, means a coming together in partnership). The intimacy implied here is expressed at the end of the Prayer of Humble Access:-

'that we may evermore dwell in Him, and He in us.'

Such union with God in Christ is the goal of our lives as Christians; in the Eucharist we are given an earthly foretaste of that heavenly banquet. We are not only reassured again of our destiny and of that ultimate wholeness which will be ours; we also begin to experience the process of healing here and now as Jesus meets us at the point of our need.

'The Meeting with The Church on Earth'. Modern liturgies rightly place an emphasis on our fellowship within the Body of Christ, the Church. The Communion table is a focus of unity for all the members of God's family; just as any family meets together for a shared meal, so the Church meets for the Eucharist. The sharing of The Peace, common practice in the majority of churches, gives physical expression to our unity in Christ.

At this point of sharing, the healing of the church community is emphasised and effected. We are reminded of the *Shalom* of the Old Testament, that peace which is God's will for his people, wholeness in community which is akin to the harmony of a choir or orchestra.

'The Meeting Point with the Church in Heaven'. Here is a 'vertical' emphasis which brings healing to the bereaved with a reminder of all those who have gone before us in the faith of Christ.

'Therefore with angels and archangels and with all the company of heaven.......'

Healing comes as we release our loved ones who have died, leaving them with God and asking him to help us with any 'unfinished business', to heal any broken relationships. There is also here a sense of timelessness and of eternity as we join the angels and the saints in worship and praise.

It has been said that *'praise is inner healing made audible'*. In the Eucharist praise and healing are the two faces of the same coin as God's people move towards wholeness in Christ. John Wardle.

CHAPTER NINE

THE HEALING OF DYING AND GRIEF

The distinguished doctor, Paul Tournier, who has written on the complementary nature of medical and spiritual has great insight into human nature. He writes that in his work with patients over the years he has found that the most tenacious of their fears is the fear of death.

This is something which the Christian faith tackles head on. St. Paul writes in 1 Corinthians 15 "Where, O death, is your sting? Thanks be to God! He gives us the victory through our Lord Jesus Christ" (NIV).

The resurrection is the way to the conquest of these fears. Psychotherapy is also a help in our understanding of attitudes towards dying and grief.

A psychotherapist puts it, "We are all sick with a terminal disease – mortality! Death is a fact of life but the manner of our death, i.e. dying, is a process shaped by cultural attitudes"[45]

He points out that in the last hundred years or so there have been changes in society which have had a deep impact on our attitudes to death and dying. Improved community health standards, the advance of medicine, better housing, the expectation of cure or entry into hospital, changes in family life which have lessened the opportunity of care for the elderly and dying at home, all have served to make death seem more remote. The dead are rapidly removed into undertakers' chapels of rest. "In today's society a silence has taken over death."

This fact makes it harder to talk in a healthy way about dying and death, and so increases the strains put upon the bereaved and those who have the care of the dying.

So often there is a pretence with the aim of sparing the patient anxiety about possible death, but this produces an unreal situation. It deprives people of opportunities of making sensible arrangements, and showing loving gratitude for each other.

The Rev. Ken Evans gives an example:-

"THE CONSPIRACY OF SILENCE
OR LET'S SPARE HIM GAME."

---

[45] A Paper by Rev. Ken Evans 'Living & Learning with the Dying', page 1.

For example, father is the patient. He realises that he is very ill, in fact dying. There are many things that he would like to discuss with his wife and children but he believes they are unaware of just how bad things are. He therefore decides to spare them this knowledge. His wife knows he is dying because the doctor has told her, and furthermore, she knows that her husband has only a very short time to live. She would like to ask her husband questions about the family finances, care of the children, ageing in-laws.

However, because she believes her husband is ignorant of the seriousness of his condition, she thinks any discussion of these important matters may frighten him or cause him 'to give in' and die all the sooner. So she, in turn, spares him, and struggles on alone. The children would like to tell their dad just how much he has meant to them and other things they never got round to telling him. However, believing that if he knew how serious the situation was it would make things even worse for him, they too decide to spare him! Everyone is convinced father does not know he is dying" (Ibid. p.3).

"In the last analysis it is our conception of death which decides or answers the questions life puts to it" (Dag Hammerskjold).

The poignancy of bereavement is well expressed by Tennyson in his poem, 'Break, Break, Break', "For O for the touch of a vanished hand and the sound of a voice that is still."

The patient will probably go through various stages of grieving about his/her forthcoming death, including anger, and then hopefully acceptance will come. "Some people never come through the depressive phase of terminal illness. Often this is where denial has been strongest, both in the patient and in those involved in his care. Time is needed to come slowly and gently to terms with the inevitable, time with others who are willing and able to listen. If that time has been given these acceptances will usually follow. This is not necessarily a happy state but the pain and struggle have gone, the fear is greatly diminished, preparations are complete and a sense of peace is present."[46]

Joy Lewis has a sense of acceptance in 'Shadowlands', the story of her remarkable marriage with C.S. Lewis and her courageous death. She, in the light of their shared Christian faith, tried to help him to face up to her impending death. She said that she was trying to get through to him that the pain then was a part of their present happiness (Shadowlands, Leonora

---

[46] The Rev. K. Evans ibid. p.9

Fleischer, Hodder Headline). In other words sorrow is part of the cost of love.

Later she was to say to him that he had to let her go. All of us in grief gradually have to let go of our loved ones and let them go to God. That is the way that we can be closest to them. It took C.S. Lewis along a hard road to come to terms with his grief over her death.

Christians find great strength in the Easter message of resurrection in Christ, but that does not lessen the pain of the temporary parting. In time he came to realise that he wasn't crying because Joy had journeyed on, but because he didn't have her any more. To live deeply is to experience both joy and sorrow deeply.

They had experienced what the Bible calls a deep one flesh union – C.S. Lewis called it 'one ship'.

"The ship of their love had had a rough passage through cruel seas. The storms were passed but they had taken their toll." "The starboard engine has gone, I, the port engine, must chug along somehow till we make harbour"[47]

In bereavement most people go through certain stages of grief. There is the initial shock, numbness and denial, 'it can't be true.' Then comes yearning involving acute emotional pain, searching with its sense of extreme loss, and anxiety. This is usually followed by anger, often repressed. People say, 'Why me?' They look for someone or something to blame. Pain is now felt as injustice. Then there is guilt, involving often doubting of faith in God, and a sense of loneliness. Some people are ostracised. Often depression ensues, with its apathy, indecisiveness and a neglect of the person's best interests. There is a crisis of identity, following the loss of marital or social status. Gradually for most some mitigating factors emerge. People gain strength to begin to come to terms with it. There is an increasing ability to say good-bye to their loved one. Acceptance slowly dawns. There is a readiness to talk more happily about the deceased. There can be deeper maturity and stronger religious faith (Rev K. Evans ibid Appendix II).

The Easter message reminds us that this life and the future life are all one in God's love. The following prayer expresses this well:-

"O God the Father Almighty, whose faithfulness never faileth: comfort, we pray thee, the souls of all who mourn; that they may abide patiently upon thee, and know that neither height nor depth, nor things

---

[47] Shadowlands, Brian Sibley, Hodder p.155, reproduced by permission of Hodder & Stoughton Ltd.

present nor things to come, nor death nor life, can separate thy children from thy love, which is in Jesus Christ thy Son our Lord. Amen."[48]

Christ's resurrection life is something to be shared here and now, and it will have its full blossoming in the life of the world to come.

Jesus says, "I am the resurrection and the life. He who believes in me will live, even though he dies: and whoever lives and believes in me will never die" (St. John 11 v.25-26 NIV).

As we look out from the sea-shore we realise that the horizon is the limit of our physical sight but that there is much more beyond the horizon. The ships as they journey out from harbour cross the horizon and go to their port of destination. So with us on the journey of life. The horizon is akin to physical death. In the power of Christ's resurrection we cross the horizon, and go to our destination, namely the heavenly city.

The following prayer expresses this well:-
"We give them back to Thee, dear Lord, Who gavest them to us. Yet as Thou didst not lose them in giving, so we have not lost them by their return. Not as the world giveth, givest Thou, O lover of souls. What Thou gavest, Thou takest not away; for what is Thine is ours always, if we are Thine. And life is eternal and love is immortal, and death is only an horizon, and an horizon is nothing save the limit of our sight. Lift us up, strong Son of God, that we may see further. Cleanse our eyes that we may see more clearly: Draw us closer to Thyself that we may know ourselves nearer to our beloved who are with Thee. And while Thou dost prepare a place for us, prepare us for that happy place that where they are and Thou art, we too may be; through Jesus Christ our Lord. Amen" (Bishop Brent).

The effect of the resurrection of Christ is to enable His love and life to be available to us at any moment, time or place. There is an ancient tradition that Pilate's wife asked the Centurion about Jesus on the afternoon of the first Good Friday:-

"Do you think Jesus is dead?"
"No, lady, I don't" is the answer.
"Then, where is He?"
"Let loose in all the world, lady, where neither Roman nor Jew nor any other man can stop the victory of His Risen Life."[49]

On the Cross, Jesus quotes from Psalm 31: "Into Thy hands I commend my spirit," a going to sleep prayer he had probably learnt as a boy. Every day is meant to be a handing over to God, the placing of ourselves into His

---

[48] E. Milner-White (Reproduced by courtesy of the Friends of York Minster).
[49] Olive Wyon, Consider Him: Three Meditations on the Passion Story S.C.M.

sure hands. Then when the time comes for us to make the final surrender in death, we shall be able to do so trustingly and lovingly. This prayer is the prayer for every crisis.

"The example and the call of the Cross alike are the continual surrender of ourselves, of all we possess, of all we would like to possess, and of all those relationships which because of our imperfect love could become possessive, and those whom we have lost awhile."[50]

Through faith in the resurrection we can be assured that we are 'in Christ'. The early Christians didn't put on their tombstones that so-and-so had died, but that so-and-so had 'entered into life'.

The Cross is the meeting place of human suffering and Divine love and interprets this mysterious union of love and suffering. The resurrection vindicates all that Jesus lived for and died for, and so assures us that none of our suffering is in vain.

Coming through trauma with God's help is like moving from death to resurrection. The Cross and the Resurrection are inseparably linked and it is the Resurrection that has the final word.

Many people in bereavement are helped by counselling.

Martin Kerry writes: -

THE HEALING OF GRIEF – THE ROLE OF COUNSELLING IN BEREAVEMENT

Bereavement as a life-crisis

A typical lifetime involves many experiences of loss such as a young person leaving home to begin an independent life, a worker leaving colleagues to move to a new job, an older person leaving their home to be cared for in an institution.

There are many more such 'life crises' involving a profound change in a person's world, bringing with them both challenges to cope and opportunities for growth.

Of all of these the experience of losing a loved one can be the most devastating and the hardest change to adjust to. For this reason many people turn to some form of counselling.

Is Counselling OK for Christians?

Some Christians are suspicious of counselling. This may be because they find it hard to ask for any form of formalised help, regarding it as a sign of weakness or lack of faith. Often those whose Christian convictions lead them to be 'care givers' find it

---

[50] In Debt to Christ p.68, Douglas Webster, Highway Press.

hardest to be 'care receivers'. Or it may be because they feel that the traditional ministry of the Church – prayer, anointing, laying on of hands – should be enough. Personally, I see it as no less appropriate for a Christian to go to a counsellor for help with the healing of heart and mind, than it would be for a Christian to go to a doctor for help with the healing of physical sickness. This in no way conflicts with the very valuable role of prayer and sacramental ministry.

Reluctance may be more easily overcome if the counsellor is also a Christian. Indeed, such a counsellor may be more readily attuned to the values and faith-world of their client, and have access to a wider range of appropriate resources such as prayers and texts. However, as with any professional, I would rather seek out a competent non-Christian than an incompetent Christian. A counsellor should be formally trained, currently supervised, and adhere to a recognised code of Ethics.

Who Needs Counselling?

The long and often painful process of grieving is a completely normal response to bereavement. It can involve initial shock and disbelief; then anger, sadness, pining, transient depression and many other changes to thoughts, feelings, and behaviour.

Not everyone will need counselling, even for such a significant life-crisis as bereavement. Support may come from a friend, family, a neighbour, a Church fellowship, a self-help group – in fact anyone who is willing to listen, to stay close and to show they care.

Counselling may be particularly needed by the vulnerable and those who have few support systems. It is also important for those whose grief becomes complicated; for example those who never begin the work of grieving, or those whose grief is still unresolved several years after their loss. Those who have been bereaved in special circumstances, such as through traumatic death or suicide are also more likely to need the help of a counsellor. Even well-supported people, whose grieving follows a normal path, may benefit from the special support available through a counsellor.

How might a Counsellor help?

William Worden in 'Grief Counselling and Grief Therapy' (Tavistock Routledge) speaks of 'the four tasks of mourning'. He characterises these as: accepting the reality of the loss, experiencing the pain of grief, adjusting to an environment where the deceased is missing, withdrawing emotional energy from the deceased and reinvesting it elsewhere.

Whilst counsellors vary in their methods and theoretical frameworks, all will broadly look to help their clients complete these four tasks. Examples of each are given below.

1. A bereaved person may be experiencing difficulty in accepting that their loved one is really gone – perhaps it is not possible to talk about the deceased without upsetting other members of the family. A counsellor may provide the opportunity to talk about the loss and what it means for the bereaved person.

2. Many of the normal feelings associated with grieving are painful and difficult to acknowledge – for example anger, guilt, anxiety, helplessness. The counsellor can provide the environment and skills to identify and facilitate expression of these feelings.

3. When someone dies the bereaved person may have lost a companion, an accountant, a gardener, a mechanic, a cook, a childminder....The counsellor may adopt a problem-solving approach to assist the bereaved person in living without the one who has died.

4. Finally, it can be hard for some bereaved people to invest energy elsewhere than in the deceased, because this can feel disloyal. A counsellor can help explore the difficulties and assist in saying a final goodbye.

SOME RESOURCES

Bereavement – Colin Murray Parkes (Penguin)
The classic text on the subject.

Letting Go – Ian Ainsworth Smith and Peter Speck (SPCK)
A guide to bereavement by two hospital chaplains.

All in the End is Harvest – ed. Agnes Whitaker (CRUSE/DLT)
An anthology of poetry and prose for the bereaved.

Counselling and Psychotherapy – Is it for Me? – British Association for Counselling (BAC)
A guide for those considering counselling.

Martin Kerry

The whole area of counselling is a 'bridge area' between medicine and the Church. It is a therapy which has grown in recent years with much greater understanding of the psychological factors in human personality and human relationships. As Bishop Morris Maddocks points out, "The aim is to render the person more secure within himself or herself."[51]

Resurrection is not just a future experience; we also experience it now. As new life comes to us through a wide variety of situations we experience resurrection.

---

[51] Morris Maddocks, The Christian Healing Ministry p.167, SPCK.

CHAPTER TEN

TENDER LOVING CARE

We often speak of people's need for T.L.C. – tender loving care. It is a therapy that can be influential in any situation however bleak the medical prognosis.

The assurance that one is loved and cared for is to journey towards wholeness in our personality.

Kathleen Ferrier, the famous contralto singer, suffered severely from cancer, but fought it with much courage and was still thankful for life's blessings. She gave much love and was surrounded by much love. As someone has written, through her wonderful art and loving nature she gave and received happiness. She would like to be thought of in a major key.

Jesus emphasises the importance of pastoral care, along with teaching, in his ministry amongst the sick. For example there is a moving passage recorded by St. Luke about the mentally ill patient who is healed by Jesus. Afterwards he is described as 'sitting at Jesus' feet, dressed and in his right mind' (St. Luke 8 v.35 NIV).

In the parable of the Good Samaritan there is clear emphasis on after-care in the provision for the wounded man. He is given to the care of the inn-keeper. "Look after him," he said, "and when I return, I will reimburse you for any extra expenses you may have" (St. Luke 10 v.325 NIV).

Again the need is shown for people to be cared for as people – on-going care. People's self-esteem is an important part of health. They need affirming as people in the love of God and not just seen as medical cases.

Every Christian is entrusted with this caring, prayerful, pastoral ministry. We can all give prayer, friendship, visiting, letter-writing, and other support to the sick. It is also two-way traffic. Again and again we receive more than we give.

"Love's strength standeth in love's sacrifice,
And whoso suffers most has most to give" (Mrs. Hamilton-King).

We can see so much of God in those who suffer as He shares supportively in their sufferings. Through the Cross Jesus shares in the reality of our pain and leads us through to resurrection.

A Vicar's wife who has been through much painful suffering writes movingly of the way in which God is with us in the pain:

"God is with us in our pain as much as He is in our rejoicing. His light shines in our darkness as well as in our day ...... when we have lost sight of Him altogether we fear Him to have withdrawn: in fact He has embedded Himself in the darkness within us where we fear even to look.......... We cannot speak of healing if we will not speak of pain. Our Lord carried His scars into resurrection and so do I."[52]

Another ministry in which suitably gifted and trained Christians can help greatly is in pastoral counselling. The pastoral care of the sick has seen many developments in recent years, with an increased sensitivity to the partnership of medical and spiritual factors. The Church is playing a fuller part in hospital life with more full-time Chaplains than ever before. Many of them are assisted by a team of trained lay visitors. Staff are much more alert to the pastoral ministry offered by the Chaplaincies both for themselves and their patients, and patients' relatives.

Here is an extract from a Chaplain's account of his work:-

Babies are born, limbs are repaired, growths are removed, organs are transplanted and minds are healed so that people can enjoy life. A Chaplain can contribute to this enjoyment of life in so many ways and help to bring the wholeness which people seek. He may be the only person giving time to a patient who just wanted to talk and talk and talk. He may be the one, as I once was, to tell a divorcee, widowed many years ago, that she **could** receive Communion after believing, mistakenly for 27 years, that her divorce meant she was barred for ever from the Sacrament. He may be the one who sits with a couple and helps them to talk about the approaching death of one of them, and what it will mean, in practical terms, for the other. He may be the one who listens as a patient expresses revulsion for his former life-style and asks to be forgiven. He may be the one to pass onto some parents the bad news their son has just received about his prognosis because he can't face telling them, something he knows will hurt them so much. He may be the one to sit at the bedside of an elderly man whose family expressed their concern for him by leaving a message which said, "Just ring and tell us when he dies, but don't disturb us during the night." He may be the one to say, casually "Well Sister, how are things?" followed by 45 minutes of nodding sympathetically while Sister tells you **exactly** how things are! Or he may be the one to hear the confession, to pronounce God's loving forgiveness, to anoint with holy oil or to share the body and blood of Christ with who knows how many Christians – faithful, lapsed, wavering,

---

[52] Jane Grayshon, "A Pathway through Pain", Hodder p.165, quoted by permission of the author.

uncertain, scared, hopeful, confident or dying. That gift of time, that sympathetic ear, that assurance of forgiveness, that willingness to stay while difficult and painful things are discussed and that sharing of God's love in his Sacraments – all these give value to the patients and their needs and help them towards abundant life which is so much more than simply 'getting better' (The Rev. Barrie Newton, Chaplain St. Mary's Hospital, London from Article in The Journal of Health Care Chaplains, June 1995).

"The mystery of human suffering – the powerlessness of handicapped people – are they more open to receive what we are trying to grasp? Are they showing us the way? In their suffering they seem to be specially precious to God, and often it is through them we receive revelations of his love…In some mysterious way the weakest lead us to God" (Jean Vanier).

Dr. Cicely Saunders has pioneered the work of hospices where particular pastoral care as well as medical care is needed to minister to patients with terminal illness. Again it is two-way traffic. "Christ is there whether He is recognised or not. The simple truths that He knows so much better than we ever can, that He knew such dependence that He even had to have His own cross carried for Him seems to have meaning for the most unaccustomed ears and to need little explanation. I believe that this is because such sufferers are in the place of his deepest identification with us all" (words of Dr Saunders quoted by her permission and published in Cicely Saunders by Shirley Du Boulay. Hodder).

Dr. Sheila Cassidy also has considerable experience of hospice work. She writes of the fact that 'no man is an island' – patients are all part of a network of relationships.   The sensitive pastoral and medical care of the dying can thus send good ripples into the life of the community as a whole. Pain can be controlled, patients' fears and anger sympathetically handled.

Some of the misunderstandings that there have been between medicine and the Church have been through wrong ideas that had their origins in Church life following the conversion of Constantine in the 4th Century. Christianity then became the official state religion and many of its problems began.

A lot of former pagans influenced Church life.

"The Graeco-Roman philosophies in which they had been brought up for many a generation had regarded sickness not as an enemy invader but as God sent! Either it was a punishment for sin or testing time for the soul's good. We have never really rid ourselves of these parasitic ideas."[53]

---

[53] The Heart of Healing, Canon George Bennett p.53 Arthur James.

Such mistaken ideas have seriously weakened the Church's pastoral ministry amongst the sick. It is only in recent times that a revival of the authentic ministry has come. Sadly some Christians still hang on to the mistaken ideas, and as a result much pastoral damage is caused.

Many patients can wrongly feel a sense of guilt or are made to feel defective in faith through these wrong notions. Such patients who need affirming in the love of God can then sadly become disillusioned with the Church.

The great antidote to fear is love as the first Epistle of St. John makes clear. "God is love. Whoever lives in love lives in God, and God in him. In this way love is made complete among us so that we will have confidence on the day of judgement because in this world we are like him. There is no fear in love but perfect love drives out fear because fear has to do with punishment. The one who fears is not made perfect in love" (1 John 4 v.16-18 NIV).

Prayerful pastoral care amidst the suffering caused by war comes over powerfully in Bishop Leonard Wilson's broadcast about his experiences as a prisoner of war. Amidst his own suffering he ministered sensitively to his fellow prisoners. "Many non-Christians came to ask me to teach them to pray, because prayer evidently meant so much to those of us who were Christians. We were not supposed to talk to each other, but when the guards were not looking I told them some of the elementary things of prayer – thanking him, being sorry for things done wrong, and praying for others. And so we formed a wider fellowship than any of us had known before, a fellowship of suffering humanity."[54]

Barrie Cooke writes:-

"We so often pay lip service to the importance of Christian fellowship. When we discover the real thing it is different to the superficial camaraderie that so often purports to be fellowship. Fellowship is as a shared way of living and loving. It is a quality of relationship governed by attitudes of mutual care and accountability, a developing openness, and a shared, prayerful attention to the person of Christ. I would say above all, that the quality of our fellowship is determined by the place we give to Jesus in our common life.

"We cannot measure how much meaningful fellowship contributes to our personal health and well being. That is not the limit of its influence. The Church's fellowship is a sign and a means of creating a new humanity. A Church intent on becoming a healing

---

[54] William Purcell, This is my Story p.112-113 Hodder 1963, reproduced by permission of David Higham Associates.

community will therefore spend much of its energies on discovering and cultivating fellowship.

"In a world where so many are 'in sorrow, need, anxiety and sickness' let us remember that our vocation, as a Church, is to replicate the ministry of Jesus." (The Rev. Barrie Cook, published in the Methodist Health and Healing Magazine 1992).

David Payne writes:-

HEALING AND PASTORAL CARE

To understand the relationship between Healing & Pastoral care one needs to look no further than the model of 'The Good Shepherd' as recorded in St. John's Gospel (chapter 10), further illustrated by reference to Ezekiel, 34, v.15-16. In these verses are clearly spelled out the seven-fold functions of the Shepherd, one of which is 'Healing'.

"I myself will be the Shepherd of the sheep, and I will make them lie down, says the Lord God. I will seek the lost, and I will bring back the strayed one, and I will bind up the crippled (or injured), and I will strengthen the weak, and the fat and the strong I will watch over. I will feed them in justice."

Here is a comprehensive summary of the Lord's care as 'Shepherd of the Flock'.

The key-point, by way of introduction, is the deep desire of the Shepherd to have a close personal knowledge of, and relationship with His sheep. "He calls his own sheep by name". (See also Isaiah 43 v.1-5.) The hallmark of Our Lord's Ministry was His deep compassion for people as individuals. He chose twelve men of very different temperament and background to be His first disciples. Much of His recorded ministry to needy folk is to **individuals.** He calls Mary by name in the Easter Garden, He returns to greet Thomas specially (John 20 v.16), on the Sunday after Easter (John 20 v.26-29). His compassion and His healing touch is for individuals. The Shepherd gets to know his sheep one by one. The ministry of pastoral care and healing asks no less of us. Each person in need is unique and special, and needs to be treated with the utmost sensitivity and respect. Above all the Shepherd longs that His sheep may come to recognise and listen to His voice (John 10 v.27). Now the seven-fold functions of the Shepherd, as spelled out by Ezekiel (Chapter 34 v.16).

1. **Restfulness** - "I will make them lie down."

There's no lovelier sight of a summer's evening in the country than to se a flock quietly at rest in a pasture while the Shepherd walks quietly among them. They are at ease because they know and trust the Shepherd. Jesus said those gracious words: "Come to me all who labour and are heavy-laden, and I will give you rest." In our pastoral care of folk in need, and in all healing ministry, be it individual ministry, or public healing services, the key-note must be quietness and tranquility, and the presentation of Christ as the One who gives rest. Isaiah 32 v.15-18 reminds us that the effect of the anointing Spirit from on high is "quietness and trust forever, and my people shall abide in a peaceful habitation, in secure dwellings and in quiet resting places." Jesus leads the flock, he never harries it!

2. **Evangelism – "I will seek the lost."**

The primary concern of the Shepherd is for the one lost sheep (Luke 15 v.3-7). Jesus' focus in this earthly ministry was for the 'outcasts', the needy, the sick, the lonely, the troubled, the poor, as a reading of the Gospels makes clear. Healing Ministry and pastoral care will rightly and inevitably follow this pattern. Jesus reminded his hearers that "Those who are well have no need of a physician, but those that are sick" (Matthew 9 v.12). The compassion of Jesus will lead us to minister largely to the afflicted. But we as 'ministers' need to recognise the 'lost areas' in all our lives, which God is continually seeking to touch and heal (e.g. painful childhood experiences). Effective healing ministry and pastoral care, sensitively exercised, will be a means of reaching many folk for Christ.

3. **Bringing back the Strayed**

Long years ago, I recall seeing a Shepherd, in Wensleydale, lifting up two ewes, which had strayed on to the narrow gated road, over the stone wall, back into their rightful pasture. Counselling, pastoral care, healing ministry is an opportunity for many to rediscover the Good Shepherd's loving arms seeking to bring them back to Himself. Walls of fear, sorrow, resentment, anger, hurt can be removed by the working of the Holy Spirit. The Shepherd can lift us up over many barriers. The deep word of the Gospel that 'it is OK to be carried' will be part of our experience, and part of our ministry. The verse in Isaiah chapter 63 verse 9 is vital. (See also the hard lesson that Peter had to learn in John 21 v.18.)

4. **Healing** – "I will bind up the crippled" (injured).

Here is a specific reference to the Healing Ministry, a ministry of 'binding up the crippled', as an integral part of the pastoral ministry, but not the sum of it. One of the most powerful accounts of the Healing Ministry comes in the Parable of the Good Samaritan (Luke 10 v.29-37). The Early Fathers saw this as a 'parable of mankind' , the wounded man in the ditch representing wounded humanity, the Good Samaritan as the figure of Christ as the loving Healer, the oil and wine as a picture of His Healing Ministry; and the 'Wayside Inn' as a picture of the local church as the caring/healing community. The ministry of Jesus was so much a ministry of 'Bandaging and pouring on oil and wine.' In our pastoral care, and in our healing ministry, we shall need to be **channels** of His Love and Grace, helping people quietly to open up to His Anointing. The Shepherd deals **gently** with His injured sheep. The use of our hands will be gentle and sensitive. There is no place for 'pushy' or careless handling. Above all we recognise we too are 'God's wounded people', allowing Him the Wounded One, to minister through us to His wounded ones.

5. Strengthening the Weak

A weak or sickly lamb may be taken into the Shepherd's home, or even the kitchen to be nourished and bottle-fed. This is a costly and particularly demanding action. Prayer and the laying-on-of-hands can bring strength and encouragement to many of God's sick people. But here is no recipe for 'quick-fix'. Pastoral care may lead us, with careful and prayerful consideration, to open our homes to needy folk. Hence the gift of the residential 'Homes of Healing' across our land.

6. Pastoral Oversight – "The fat and the strong I will **watch** over." The Good Shepherd is ever vigilant, watching over His flock by day and night. In our caring and healing ministry we need to have the gift of sight and in-sight which Jesus had. "Behold an Israelite in whom is no guile," said Jesus about Nathanael, whom he had never met previously (John 1 v.47). The pastor, or the 'pastoral care team' will need the gifts of the Holy Spirit as they watch over the flock. (See the 'Charismata' in 1 Corinthians 12.)

7. Feeding – "And I will **feed** them…"

Many who come to the Church or the Pastor for help, will be emotionally and spiritually hungry and thirsty. Jesus alone can feed them, so they will need the Ministry of Word and Sacrament. How vital that we share the Scriptures with those whom we seek to pastor. How inadequate, even dangerous, is any healing ministry divorced from clear biblical teaching. How impoverished the sheep if they have not learned to feed upon CHRIST in word and Sacrament. The Chief Shepherd's commission was to **preach** the

Gospel and **heal** the sick (Luke 9 v.2, Luke 10 v.9), a two-fold commission which at our peril do we separate.

Thus in summary can we see the relationship of the Healing Ministry and Pastoral Care. Healing Ministry, in all its aspects, will be **allied** with, and **part** of our Pastoral care. A careful study of Ezekiel 34 and John chapter 10, will refresh our minds on this. Above all we need to be reminded this is not our Ministry but **HIS.** The healing of the lame man in Acts 3 is a powerful reminder of this. And when all our efforts fail, we need to hear again Jesus' words in John 5 v.17 **"My Father is working and I am working still."**

David Payne (Warden of the Crowhurst Home of Healing 1978-1984.)

The World Health Organisation definition of health (1948) says: "Health is a state of complete physical, mental and social well being and not merely the absence of illness."

Relationships are therefore a key factor in health, our relationship with God and with one another. Our main motivation for caring is that God cares. God's care truly values people as people, is not patronising, nor bossy, nor possessive, unlike some wrongly motivated human care. To serve others most effectively we must first let ourselves be cleansed and motivated by God.

"So in consequence your own service of humanity is a service humble, unselfconscious, unpatronising. It will meet the needs of humanity more deeply, since God has first been allowed to meet your deepest need."[55]

There is a mysterious union between love and suffering. This is focused in the Cross of Jesus. A famous modern doctor with a long experience of pastoral care for his patients probes into the reason why some situations are negative, some positive, in suffering. Doctor Paul Tournier writes in his book 'Creative Suffering' (SCM Press). He feels that love is the key factor. "Deprivations without the aid of love spell catastrophe", while "the decisive factor in making deprivation bear fruit is love" (p. 34).

---

[55] Michael Ramsey, Introducing the Christian Faith S.C.M. p.94.

MOORLEY'S

are growing Publishers, adding several new titles to our list each year. We also undertake private publications and commissioned works.

Our range of publications includes: **Books of Verse**
Devotional Poetry
Recitations
Drama
Bible Plays
Sketches
Nativity Plays
Passiontide Plays
Easter Plays
Demonstrations
Resource Books
Assembly Material
Songs & Musicals
Children's Addresses
Prayers & Graces
Daily Readings
Books for Speakers
Activity Books
Quizzes
Puzzles
Painting Books
Daily Readings
Church Stationery
Notice Books
Cradle Rolls
Hymn Board Numbers

Please send a S.A.E. (approx 9" x 6") for the current catalogue or consult your local Christian Bookshop who should stock or be able to order our titles.